A History of
Newtownbutler

A History of
Newtownbutler

Barbara Chapman

NONSUCH

First published 2005

Nonsuch Publishing Limited
73 Lower Leeson Street
Dublin 2
Ireland
www.nonsuch-publishing.com

National Library Cataloguing in Publication Data.
A catalogue record for this book is available from the National Library.

ISBN 1 84588 525 2

Typesetting and origination by Tempus Publishing Limited.
Printed in Great Britain.

Contents

Acknowledgements

It is impossible to remember all the people who have contributed to this book, but I would like to thank the following for their help.

The Rt. Hon. Earl of Erne, the Rt. Hon. Earl of Lanesborough, Lt. Col. Butler, The Revd Canon E. Murphy, The late Very Revd Nevil O'Neill, Former Dean of Clogher , The Revd Canon John Hay , The Revd Nigel Baylor The Revd Dudley Cooney, The Staff of the County Museum, The Staff of the Lisnaskea Library, Fermanagh District Council Community Relations Department, Mrs Joan Allen, Mrs Anderson, Miss Margery Armstrong, Mr Wm. Allen, Mr Walter Brady, Mrs Marjorie Burke, Mr Francis Fitzpatrick, Mr Thomas Gunn, Mr Sam Hutchinson, Mrs Hamilton-Johnston, The late Miss Molly Johnston, Mr and Mrs W. B. Loane, Miss Erica Loane, Mr Wm Little, Mr Arthur Maguire, Mr John Maguire, Mr Noel Maguire, Miss Doreen Moore, Mr Philip Moore, Mr Jimmy Morgan, Mrs Mary Frances Murray, Mr Eamon McCabe, Mr Eugene McCabe, Mr and Mrs Sam McCoy, Mr J. J. McCusker, Mr Fergus McQuillan, Miss Brigid O'Reilly, Mr Bert Robinson, Mr and Mrs Ryan (Crom), Mr Scan Sharkey, Mrs Maggie Wilson, Mr Phillip Wilson

Finally, may I thank Miss Rona Kelly and Mrs Lorna Elliott who typed the original scripts and the staff at Trimbles who gave valuable advice in the printing of the final text.

Barbara Chapman
Newtownbutler Local History Project Committee

Foreword

'NEW-TOWN-BUTLER!' the railway porter's call had an anvil's ring about it! At least that's how it sounded to me some fifty years ago on the north bound train from Dublin as it came to a clanking standstill at the Station.

Some years later, when I became a Road Surveyor in my native Fermanagh, I discovered that names like McAvinney and McQuillan were well-known in Newtownbutler as well as the Johnstons and the Hutchinsons — all equally proud of their hometown.

It was only in more recent years, however, in my more leisurely days of retirement, that I have found time to take a good look around the place and its fine buildings. On a hill to the south stands St Mary's Roman Catholic Church with its attractive altar area, adorned with glowing figures in stained glass and embellished with simple furnishings of solid granite. It is complemented on the northern skyline by St Comgall's Church of Ireland with its four wide transepts in the form of a Greek Cross, under an exquisitely decorative ceiling.

A few miles to the west are the lakeside environs of Crom Castle, a superb area for walking and now managed by the National Trust. Also in the grounds of Crom is the birthplace of Erne Laureate, novelist Shan Bullock.

Barbara Chapman has spent all her adult life at Newtownbutler. When she mentioned to me that she and some of her friends were planning a book on the local history of the area, I was elated at the prospect. Barbara, already an esteemed schoolteacher and youth leader, soon became one of the stalwarts of the Fermanagh Field Club when it was founded in 1956 — I cannot think of anyone more suitable to compile this 'Aladdin's Cave' of delights, gleaned from in and around Newtownbutler.

I have already been privileged to read the book in its first draft and I was unable to leave it down until I had reached the last page.

Here we have rousing sagas of ancient battles, early photographs depicting school days and fair days, as well as people and buildings and memories of the American troops billeted here in wartime. Each page sparkles with something interesting, we learn that the first Gaelic Football Club in Fermanagh was founded here over a hundred years ago, social changes recall Kate McKeever's sweet shop which sold 'gob-stoppers' which changed colours as you sucked one for up to half an hour!

The Old Station House, Newtownbutler

Trusting you will find similar rewards for yourself . . .
Authors, sponsors and publishers have combined to make this book a credit to Newtownbutler.

Walter Brady

Main Street, Newtownbutler

From Main Street looking along the Crom Road, Newtownbutler

one

Introduction

Newtownbutler and district is situated in the south east corner of County Fermanagh on the main road from Enniskillen to Dublin, about seventeen miles from Enniskillen. The next largest town is the region of Lisnaskea, about five miles to the north. The Border of the Republic of Ireland is about four miles away with Clones being the nearest town. Newtownbutler is about four miles from the famous Lough Erne, which means that it shares with many other regions in County Fermanagh one of the finest natural beauty spots in Ireland.

The town of Newtownbutler is situated on a small hill about 300 feet high and consists mainly of two streets, High Street and Main Street, the former being the main Enniskillen to Dublin Road and the latter the road to and from Clones in County Monaghan. The main part of the town lies on the north side of the river, which emerges from the hillside at Fuaran more, which means 'the Big Spring' in the townland of Tully. It is not clear when Newtownbutler began as a town. As the name suggests it was a 'planter town' built on the estate of Leitrim, granted to Sir John Wishart. Wishart sold it eventually to Sir Stephen Butler who came to Ireland in the reign of James I and who owned 1,500 acres in an area about a mile north of the present town as well as a large grant of confiscated land in County Cavan. It is not unreasonable to suppose that Newtownbutler, like Belturbet in County Cavan, owes it's origin to Sir Stephen Butler. In 1622 the town was said to have ten English families. We know from Church records that a Church was built there in 1629 with a surrounding churchyard. The clear sign that it was a plantation town is shown by its cross shape and wide streets.

Like all 'Newtowns', we may ask what was there before the town was built? This is not clear but the town was built partly on the townland of Achadh Ge, or Aghagay as it has come to be spelt, which means 'the field of the geese'. It may well have been a market centre before the early seventeenth century and got it's name from the number of geese bought and sold there. But the weakness of this theory is that there is only a small river running through Newtownbutler, so connection by water, so important in olden times, was not very satisfactory. There is an argument for saying that the forerunner of Newtownbutler as the main settlement in this area was an area called 'Wattlebridge'. Wattlebridge, a few miles further south, on the road to Dublin had a ford across the Finn River for heavy traffic and a bridge of wattles for pedestrian use only. Wattlebridge had also great possibilities of connection by water and was in fact linked with many

Newtownbutler, Looking out at Main Street

towns in the early eighteenth century. Wattlebridge was also within easy reach of Galloon, on the Erne, where the monastery was situated. From early times signs of its habitation are shown by the 'Druids Temple', more of which we will hear later. The present site of Newtownbutler may well have been chosen by Sir Stephen because he owned the lands and the coach road through this area was becoming more important.

We don't know for sure which theory is correct or if either of them is close to the mark, but it is interesting to speculate.

There are two other important dates in later history, which we can be sure of and for which Newtownbutler is memorable. In 1641 the rebellion by Rory O'Neill forced many of the townspeople to seek refuge in the church.

It seems that many of the settlers lost their lives in this event. In 1689 the Battle of Newownbutler took place giving the forces of William III a very significant victory over the forces of James II. The importance of this victory in the history of Ireland cannot be underestimated, as will be seen later in this book.

Newtownbutler therefore has a very interesting past and is a mixture of the Planter and the Gael. Like all towns in Ireland it has its own particular character and it is hoped that this book will uncover for the reader many of the hidden treasures of this little town in south eastern Fermanagh.

two

The Butler Family

Col. Butler who used to live at Inish Rath has been a great help in supplying information about his family for this section. The Butler family, in the past, was very interested in the town and it is most likely that the town derives its name of Newtownbutler from the investments of that family. Many of the residents came from Belturbet where the Butlers resided at Lanesborough Lodge.

The Rt. Hon. Humphrey Butler, third Baron Newtownbutler and second Viscount, was created Earl of Lanesborough in 1756. He was Member of Parliament for Belturbet.

The Lanesboroughs owned considerable property in different parts of Ireland. By the beginning of the twentieth century, Lanesborough Lodge was only occupied during the summer. There was keen sailing on Upper Lough Erne until the outbreak of the 1914 war. Immediately after Cowes week (Isle of Wight) the Upper Lough Erne Yacht Club burst into activity centred on Crom. Many of the sailors came regularly. House parties took place at the big houses of Crom, Castle Saunderson, St Hubert's, Rossferry, Inish Rath and Lanesborough Lodge. This was before the Galloon Bridge and the 'New Bridges' were built and the surface of the lake was unobstructed. Lt. Col. Butler's grandfather built the house on Inish Rath about 1850 and the family lived there until 1951.

The Earldom will inevitably become extinct within the foreseeable future as the present Earl has one daughter and no sons. Lt. Col. Butler is the heir. He had three sons, unfortunately two died in infancy and the third was tragically killed in a train crash along with his mother, née Ruth Barton, of the Waterfoot, near Kesh.

Lanesborough Lodge was burnt down about 1922. Lord Lanesborough still owns property in the Newtownbutler area, with devaluation; it amounts to very little financial gain.

Reilly's Hotel was called 'The Lanesborough Arms' and it had a stained-glass panel above the main door depicting the coat of arms of the Lanesboroughs, until the big bomb of 1974 destroyed many buildings in the town.

The history of the Butlers would not be complete without recording the following, which concerns St Ann's Parish Church in Dublin. There is a tradition that St Ann and her husband were bakers and on the entablatures at the front doors there is the likeness of two-penny loaves. Possibly this may have suggested a plan to Theophilus, Baron Newtownbutler to make a bequest to help feed the poor of St Ann's Parish. There are shelves in the Church where loaves are

The Butler Family Crest

Crom Castle – an architectural beauty of Newtownbutler's past heritage

placed and beneath these shelves is an inscription which reads....'The Rt. Hon. Theophilus Lord Newtown of Newtown Butler Bequeathed to the Poor of St Ann's Parish for ever, Thirteen (13) pounds per annum to be distributed in bread at Five Shillings Each Week'. The date of the inscription is 1723. This was paid regularly until 1895, when estates were sold and £300 was invested. Each weekend the Bequest is still honoured ... a small token of the past. To this day a few loaves are available, after evening services each Sunday or early Monday to deserving persons without religious distinction.

three

The Island of Galloon

Galloon Island, as it is known locally, is situated two and a half miles south west of Newtownbutler and is the first of the ninety islands with which Upper Lough Erne is studded. It is connected to the mainland from the townland of Derrydoon by a bridge, which was built in the early 1930s. There are several farms on the island and at the beginning of the sixth century a monastic settlement was founded by Saint Tighernach, as has had been detailed elsewhere in the history of the parish of Galloon. On this island is an ancient cemetery which along with the early monastic foundation is not as well known as it deserves to be. This may be partly explained because of its isolated location but it doesn't explain the fact that it was not until the 1960s that archaeologists began to examine this site in detail.

There is little left to be seen except the much worn shafts of two Celtic crosses. We know little of the early history of the monastery but the Annals of Ulster relate that in 836 AD 'the churches of Lough Erne were destroyed by the Gentiles' and in all probability Galloon would not have escaped. The sculptured crosses, which date from the end of the ninth of the beginning of the tenth century, show that the monastery must have been in a flourishing, condition at the time they were erected. The Church, which later succeeded the Monastery on Galloon Island, was destroyed during the Cromwellian wars and the two high crosses were damaged also. The stones of the church were used to build the present surrounding wall and nothing remains except the head and sill of one of its ancient windows.

Of the two Celtic crosses mentioned earlier, one is inside the east cemetery gate and the other is situated at the opposite western boundary.

The East Cross

The base consists of a single stone, divided into two parts, wider at the bottom than the top, without any sculpture. The east face of the shaft contains four panels, two of which show interlaced knots and the other two the sacrifice of Isaac on the bottom panel and Moses with Aaron and Heir on the third panel. The west face of the East Cross is made up of three panels showing from the bottom upwards; the Adoration of the magi, the Baptism of Christ and St Paul and St Anthony receiving the bread from the raven. The north face of the East Cross contains three .. The figures are very worn and difficult to interpret. The bottom panel may depict Jacob wrestling with the angel or it may depict the return of the Prodigal son. The centre and top panels depict the Resurrection and the Last Judgement and the two animals shown on the centre are a sheep and a goat, symbolical of the saved and the lost.

The south side of the East Cross shaft is made up of a fret and spiral design covering two thirds of the face. The top of the panel contains the figures of an animal, head downwards, though some people regard it as depicting the crucifixion of St Peter, who tradition says, was crucified head downwards as he did not deem himself worthy of being crucified like our Lord. Still others think it represents the Massacre of the Innocents.

At the bottom of the south side of the East Cross under favourable lighting conditions, a much-defaced inscription may be seen. It is extremely difficult to decipher, but seems to read; 'Maelechiavain', in ancient Irish lettering. Bearing in mind the close connection between Galloon and Clones in the ninth and tenth centuries, it is possible that this cross may be a memorial to Maelciavain, abbot of Clones and bishop of Armagh, who is recorded in the Annals of Ulster to have died in 914 AD.

If this surmise be correct it furnishes satisfactory evidence for dating the age of this memorial.

The cross and head of this cross are missing from the shaft. Part of a mutilated head lying in the cemetery will be described later.

Galloon West Cross

The base of this cross is similar to that of the East Cross base and shaft and measures about six feet. The east face of the shaft contains three panels. The bottom panel contains three figures and may depict the arrest of Christ. Daniel in the Lion's den is shown on the middle panel. Adam and Eve under the tree of knowledge are shown on the top panel. The west face of this shaft contains three panels, the bottom one depicting, 'The Three in the Fiery Furnace', the central one depicting 'Noah's Ark'.

The north side of this shaft shows at the bottom a spiral pattern, in the centre an animal head downwards and at the top two dragons.

The south side of the shaft of the west cross shows on the top panel, David breaking the jaws of a lion. Underneath this panel are two human figures, too defaced to be identified. The second panel seems to depict Jacob wrestling with the angel. In the bottom panel there is an almost obliterated inscription in ancient Irish lettering which seems to read 'Dublitir'. The Annals of the Four Masters and of Ulster record the death of a certain Dublitir, an historian and Abbot of Clones monastery, in 877 or 879 AD. This again shows that these crosses were probably erected in the ninth or tenth century.

Galloon Cross Head and Ring

These fragments lie at present at the base of the West Cross, but it is more likely that they belong to the East Cross as Daniel in The Lion's Den, which figures on this head piece, is already depicted on the shaft of the West Cross. The portion of the Cross Head still to be had consists of part of the centre, one arm and a small section of the ring. The arm shows that the width of the unbroken cross was three feet six inches. The Crucifixion, the arrest of Christ and Daniel in the Lion's Den are depicted on the surviving parts of this Cross Head. The section of the ring of the Cross Head is ornamented with knots and an interlaced border.

Another interesting feature of graveyards like Galloon is the very interesting carving on the gravestones. In the east part of Fermanagh at Pubble, Aghalurcher and Galloon, the stone carvers produced a very distinctive type of gravestone bearing the emblems of man's mortality. These symbols can include such items as a skull and crossed bones, a sand timer, a bell or a coffin. These symbols are found on earlier tombstones made for the new plantation families of the area. The tombstones are said to date from the late seventeenth century onwards and are also to be found in Magheraveely, Old Drummully and Newtownbutler graveyards and others no doubt in the wider area.

Returning to the island itself, during the 1980s, a small lay-by and jetty were built to accommodate tourists and local people. Many children learned to swim on the Derrydoon side of the bridge; the nearest swimming pool was in Belfast! Children also liked to hunt for fresh water mussels, which were to be found in the mud on the Galloon side of the bridge. During the 1930s the Parish Priest, Canon Maguire had water sports at Derrydoon.

The Royal Society of Antiquaries of Ireland (1934) have published photographs in their Journal. Galloon Island is therefore well worth a visit, to explore and examine these interesting remains of early Irish Christianity.

four

Crom Castle

Crom Castle is the most famous historic building in the immediate Newtownbutler area. One can drive to it from the centre of the town, turning at the crossroads along the Crom Road, which leads through another crossroads almost directly to the front gates. Crom Castle is situated on the east side of Upper Lough Erne and was the seat of Abraham Crichton Esq. It is built on a flat piece of ground commanded by hills, which are covered with dense woods.

The exquisite interspersion of water, hills, islands, woods and lawns from a landscape, which is hard to excel.

The name 'Crom' means 'sloping' or 'crooked' and is supposed to refer to the winding of the Erne River at this point.

In 1610, the land then owned by the Maguires was granted to Michael Balfour, Lord of Mountwhany in Fifeshire, under the plantation scheme of Ulster and 1,500 acres lying around Crom, including some of the islands. He commenced the erection of the Castle or fortress in 1611 by cutting down two hundred oaks.

The terms of this grant required the holder to farm 450 acres directly and to build a fortified residence or Castle on the land. When Michael Balfour arrived with 'eight freeholders and leaseholders and four women servants' he began building a Castle close to the shore on the south side of the townland.

In 1616, Michael Balfour sold the property to Sir Stephen Butler, who completed the Castle at great expense. The present dimensions are about fifty feet square, but early descriptions of the fortress describe it as consisting of an outer enclosure or 'bawne' sixty feet square, with a twenty-two feet square lime and stone house within the enclosure.

Crom was leased in 1624 to the Protestant Bishop of Clogher, Dr James Spottiswood. About the time of the 1641 Rebellion it was held by the McManuses. On Dr James Spottiswood's death in 1644, he bequeathed the Castle to his children, one of whom, Mary married Abraham Crichton in 1655. Thus the leasehold passed to that family. It was afterwards converted into a perpetuity, subject to a small head rent, which was bought out by the Earl of Erne in 1810 from Brinsley, fourth Earl of Lanesborough, a descendent of Francis Butler.

Abraham Crichton was MP for Lifford and among the heirlooms preserved at Crom are maces and Borough book of the Corporation of Lifford.

Crom Castle, Newtownbutler as it stands today

It was during his time that Crom was besieged. As it commanded the waterway between Belturbet and Enniskillen, Crom was a place of considerable importance. In the struggle for the Crown between James and William, Crom was twice unsuccessfully besieged, first by Lord Galmoy in 1689 and later by Lord Mountcashel. Colonel Abraham Crichton had a son, David, who was a lad of eighteen years and who greatly distinguished himself during the two sieges of Crom Castle.

Colonel Abraham Crichton also distinguished himself whilst commanding a Regiment of Foot at the Battle of Aughrim. He was High Sheriff and MP for County Fermanagh in 1673 and 1692 and MP for the Borough of Enniskillen in 1695.

He died in 1706 and was succeeded by his grandson, John Crichton. He died in 1716 and was buried in Newtownbutler. He confirmed the succession of the Estate to his uncle, David.

David was the fifth and youngest son of Colonel Abraham Crichton. He was MP for Augher, County Tyrone and afterwards for the Borough of Lifford.

He died on 1 June 1728 and was succeeded by Abraham, the only surviving son, who was advanced to the peerage of Ireland by the title, Baron Erne of Crom Castle, in 1768.

He died in 1722 having directed that he should be buried temporarily at St Andrew's Church, Dublin and afterwards in the vault ordered by him to be built in Newtownbutler. This vault can be seen today standing on the south wing of the Church of Ireland Parish Church of Galloon. It was during his lifetime in 1764, that the Castle was accidentally destroyed by fire. After the old Castle was burnt the family lived mostly in Dublin and only occasionally visited Crom, probably staying with Abraham's sister, Meliora Ward, who lived at Knockballymore.

Abraham was succeeded by his second son, John, born in 1731. He was advanced in the peerage by the title, Viscount Erne, in 1780 and in 1789, became the first Earl of Erne. He was elected one of the Irish Representative Peers in the Imperial Parliament in 1800.

He left £20,000 for the erection of a new Castle. The foundation was laid in 1832 and the building completed by Colonel John Crichton, afterwards third Earl of Erne.

Edward Blore (an English Architect) was employed to draw up plans for a castellated Tudor revival mansion in 1830 which was finally completed in 1838. About 1840, The Turf House and Stable and Coach Yard were completed. The White Bridge to Inisherk allowed access to the newly built walled garden on the island.

Much of the new Castle was destroyed by fire in 1841. The Castle was rebuilt, along with a new boathouse for the use of the Lough Erne Yacht Club.

John died in 1828 and was buried in Newtownbutler. He was succeeded by his second son, John Crichton, born 1772. By his marriage to Jane Weldon, he merged Aghalane Manor in the Estate of the Ernes. He died in 1833 and was buried in Newtownbutler.

His eldest son, John, succeeded his uncle Abraham, second Earl of Erne, in 1842. He was created Peer of the United Kingdom in 1876 by the title, Lord Fermanagh of Lisnaskea in County Fermanagh. He died at Crom in 1885 and was buried in the Chancel of the Church of the Holy Trinity at Crom.

He was succeeded by John Henry, third Earl of Erne, who was born in October 1839 and educated at Eton and Christ Church, Oxford. He was High Sheriff of Fermanagh in 1864 and of Donegal in 1867. He was also MP for Enniskillen and Fermanagh. He was elected three times Chairman of Fermanagh County Council between 1899 and 1908.

John Henry was succeeded by his son, Henry, who was killed in the war in 1914.

The late Lord Erne (John) was killed in the last war, in 1940, leaving a family of three. Henry Crichton is the present incumbent and his son John is the heir.

On 18 November 1940, the Castle and part of the Estate was requisitioned by the War Department and troops took possession on 6 April 1941. The Officers lived in the Castle and the men lived in Nissan Huts. The Seaforth Highlanders were the first to arrive (Malcolm Marshall's father was one of these), followed by the 6th Battalion, Royal Berkshire Regiment. In 1942, the Camp was occupied by the USA Army. The Estate was returned to the Erne family in 1946.

The modern Castle of Crom stands on a hill on a narrow peninsula, a short distance away from the old Castle.

In Crom may be seen, the largest area of semi-woodland left in the North of Ireland, making it a naturalist's paradise. Detailed surveys have been carried out by botanists and conservationists.

One of the most significant spectacles in the Estate is 'The Colouries'.
In the spring, there is a carpet of bluebells interspersed with the glowing colour of rhododendrons and azaleas.

Close by the ruins of the Old Castle are the remains of a seventeenth century formal garden and bowling green enclosed by a battlemented ha-ha. During the years after the Second World War, this area was used by various Youth Organisations as a camping ground.

To the south of the old fortress along the lake shore in the centre of the walled garden is the old giant Florencecourt yew, hundreds of years old. The straight branches ascend to a height of twenty-five feet while the trunk of the tree is twelve feet in girth and the horizontal branches form a circle over a hundred feet in circumference. It forms a shade impenetrable by the heaviest rain. There is a tradition that an O'Neill attainted for rebellion in the reign of Queen Elizabeth, previous to his departure for Spain, took leave of his lady love under the old yew tree.

The Crom Church built by the Crichton family across the water at Derryvore is reached by a short boat journey or sixteen mile journey by land. It is in the Diocese of Kilmore and services are taken by the Rector of Derrylin.

The Crichton Tower on Gad Island was built in 1847. There is a hexagonal Summer House near the lough where the family took afternoon tea. The large walled garden was in use till

The Tea House, Crom, Newtownbutler

about the middle of the century and people always enjoyed a visit to the gardens to buy fresh fruit and vegetables. The produce was taken to Ward's shop in Enniskillen by Mr Hislop, the head gardener. Mr Jackson was also a Gardener of renown who worked there. His son opened a shoe shop in Enniskillen and this is still being carried on by members of the family.

The following is an extract from the Belfast Newsletter of Wednesday, 21 November 1928 supplied by Mrs Ryan of Crom concerning the 21st birthday celebrations of the Earl of Erne at Crom Castle:-

'The Earl stepped from a train at Newtownbutler to find the platform crowded with inhabitants from the district anxious to give him a hearty welcome to his country seat. He is almost six feet in height, well built and carries himself like a soldier. That is as it should be, for he is an Officer of the Royal Horse Guards Blue. He was wearing a navy blue suit, overcoat of similar colour and a bowler hat. Then Dr J. C. Fitzgerald, representing a committee of the residents of Newtownbutler stepped forward and read an address of welcome.

Dr Fitzgerald then handed to Lord Erne a gold watch, as a token of the esteem and regard in which he was held by the people of the district. Lord Erne thanked the people and said he would treasure it very highly. The Earl then entered a motor car and was driven through Newtownbutler, which was decorated, to Crom Castle. At the entrance gates he was welcomed by flute bands and drumming parties from Crom, Gortgorgan and Glassmullough.

Other celebrations included; bonfires, singsongs and presentations.'

In 1987, part of the Estate was taken over by the National Trust and opened to the public from late spring to autumn. This has resulted in many improvements, not least the fact that many of the estate houses have been restored to their original state, thus preserving the character of the Estate. Newtownbutler is very fortunate to have such a marvelous and unique tourist attraction on its doorstep.

five

The Battle of Newtownbutler

During the wars of the revolution 1688-91 when James II and William III fought for the throne of England and both made use of Ireland as a pawn in the game of battle, the district of Newtownbutler and Wattlebridge played a conspicuous part, in what is known as the siege and gallant defence of Enniskillen, scarcely less memorable than the siege and defence of Derry.

It is as well to recall the main events in this epic struggle. In December 1688, the Enniskilleners had commenced their insurrection by refusing to admit into the town two companies of Sir Thomas Newcomen's Regiment of Foot, sent to quarter there. They continued to arm daily and in April of 1689 they rejected the terms of surrender offered to them from King James by Brigadier Pierce Butler, Third Lord Galmoy. That officer then tried to secure by strategy the Castle of Crom, a frontier post of the enemy, but was forced to withdraw without affecting anything.

The task of reducing all the Enniskilleners to obedience was then assigned to Lieutenant General Justin McCarthy, recently created Lord Mountcashel. He assembled his troops at Belturbet and proceeded on the 7 August 1689 to Crom Castle which was defended by Governor Crichton, which held out stubbornly against all the assaults of the Jacobite forces. Messengers were sent to inform the governor of Enniskillen of the attack on Crom Castle and about the same time the news came to Enniskillen that McCarthy had sent part of his army to take Lisnaskea, a town of some strength about ten miles from Enniskillen.

Colonel Wolseley in charge of the Enniskilleners sent Lieutenant-Colonel Berry with seven or eight troops of horse, three foot companies and two troops of dragoons to Lisnaskea as McCarthy was said to be about to station a garrison in the Castle of Lisnaskea.

When he arrived he found no one there and simply encamped all night in the open fields. Next day he marched his men from Lisnaskea towards Newtownbutler and Crom Castle. Berry sent scouts ahead of the forces to discern the size and nature of opposition. At Donagh the scouts caught sight of the opposition and Berry himself, in retreat, discovered from a high vantage point that they were double the size of his own forces. Berry withdrew his forces to the end of a narrow road, which ran through a bog about a mile from Lisnaskea.

Colonel Anthony Hamilton who led General McCarthy's forces advanced to attack. The Jacobite forces were driven back and Berry's army forced them into a hasty retreat. Berry recalled his men when news came to him that McCarthy was advancing with his main body. In this encounter the Jacobite forces lost two hundred men and thirty prisoners were taken.

Later that morning Colonel Wolseley arrived at Lisnaskea to support Berry and to congratulate him. In their haste to come quickly they had brought no provisions but when they were asked whether they would retreat to Enniskillen or advance to fight, they all agreed unanimously to advance and fight.

The army now under Wolseley and Berry numbered over 2,000 men while McCarthy had left Dublin ten days before with 3,600 men under his command.

The Jacobite forces having advanced to meet the Williamite forces retreated to within half a mile of Newtownbutler. They retreated to a narrow stretch of road, which ran through a bog at the base of a hill. They were obviously in a very good position to defend against the advancing forces.

The Williamite forces seeing the obvious danger split their foot soldiers to the right and left of this narrow road while Berry advanced with the horse soldiers in the centre along this road, with Wolseley and the main body bringing up the rear. The Jacobite forces opened fire on the advancing Williamite army who for their part did not break ranks in their steady march.

The Williamite forces began to return fire and witnessed quite quickly the steady retreat of the Jacobite forces who as they retired set fire to the town of Newtownbutler and the country houses which lay around it.

Both armies passed through Newtownbutler and had gone nearly a mile beyond when they came to another bog through which a narrow road passed as before and on the rising ground at the other end of this causeway the main body of the Jacobite army was drawn up in order of battle. The Jacobite horsemen were on the hill, while the foot soldiers, a little further down, were posted mostly under cover. The Williamite forces advanced as before with the foot soldiers taking the bog and the horsemen keeping the road. The cannon of the Jacobite forces kept the horsemen back but the foot soldiers of the Williamite army advanced steadily under fire and seized the cannon and beat the ground forces out of their positions before commencing deliberately to ascend the hill. No sooner were the cannon silenced, than the Williamite horsemen dashed over the causeway at speed to take their part in the battle.

When the Jacobite horsemen, from the top of the hill, saw that the bog had been crossed and the guns captured, they wheeled about and galloped off in the direction of Wattlebridge, leaving their foot soldiers to fend for themselves. When the Jacobite forces saw the retreat of their horsemen, they too broke and fled. It may interest the reader to know that the great bog mentioned here is situated in the townlands of Kilgarrett and part of Aughnahinch.

The reputed road or causeway through the bog was levelled some years ago as part of a land reclamation scheme. In the process the road called locally 'McCarthy's Road' was taken away and in another development a well, known as 'McCarthy's Well' was filled in. As we return to the Battle of Newtownbutler, we recall that when the Jacobite foot soldiers retreated taking the route to the right of the causeway to the banks of Lough Erne they threw their weapons into the turf pits as they went. The Williamite foot soldiers followed and their opponents, in desperation took to the Lough with only one out of 500 surviving. This place which lies between Inisfendra in County Fermanagh and Derryvona in County Cavan has since been known as the 'Bloody Pass' and a heap or mound in Derryvona townland, known as 'Galloon' (not to be confused with Galloon Island) marks the place where the bodies of some of the slain were interred.

In retrospect it seems strange that the Jacobite horsemen fled without a fight. Within a few weeks after the Battle of Newtownbutler, one of the chaplain's in King William's army was informed that the whole affair was caused by an officer mistaking the word of command. When the Williamite forces attacked forcefully on the right wing of MacCarthy's army, he ordered

The Old Mile Stone at Crom Cross

some of his men to face the right and march to the support of their colleagues. The officer who received the order in the heat of the moment did not fully understand the command and ordered his men to face right about and march. When the men on the hill saw their own soldiers turning towards them, they concluded they were retreating and turned themselves in order to retreat. The Williamite horsemen from Enniskillen pursued the Jacobite horsemen for ten miles but failed to overtake them and planted a guard at Wattlebridge to secure that pass. Colonel McCarthy, though wounded, had his life spared and was taken to Enniskillen as a prisoner. Captain Cooper of the Enniskilleners spared his life as it was known that on a previous occasion he had intervened to save the life of Colonel Crichton when he was at the mercy of Galmoy.

McCarthy later escaped and in later years in the service of France commanded the famous 'Mountcashel Brigade'.

Among the trophies and memorials of the Battle of Newtownbutler is the armour worn by McCarthy when he fought at Kilgarrett, Newtownbutler a place still known as 'Battle Hill'. This is preserved at Crom Castle.

This was by far the greatest victory yet obtained by the Williamites on the field of battle, since the commencement of the war.

Two thousand amateur soldiers at Enniskillen had in battle defeated nearly double that number of Jacobite forces.

When the remnant of McCarthy's army reached Dublin, it was found that 3,000 of those who had left it only two weeks before were missing.

Two thousand were actually slain, five hundred drowned in Lough Erne and four hundred were taken prisoners, most of whom were officers. On the side of the Enniskilleners, there were only twenty killed and forty or fifty wounded. It was not until two or three days afterwards that the Enniskilleners learned that the day of their victory at Newtownbutler was the very day on which the army of King James had retreated from Derry. The 31 July 1689 was therefore a memorable day in the history of the conflict between James II and William III in Ireland which had its climax at the Battle of the Boyne in the following year.

six

'Wattlebridge' and 'the Druid's Temple'

The name Wattlebridge is derived from the type of bridge that was first used to cross the Finn River at this point. It was a wooden structure of wattles or bent rods for use by pedestrians only. Heavy traffic crossed the river at a shallow ford nearby. A stone bridge now spans the Finn River and connects the townlands of Annaghmore and Edergool, but the name associated with the original bridge has been retained. It has given its name to the townland of Edergool, which is now commonly known as Wattlebridge.

The line of the old road from Cavan to Lisnaskea via Wattlebridge may still be traced for miles.

One hundred years ago, Wattlebridge was one of the stopping stages on the Dublin-Enniskillen Mail Coach route. The 'Down' mail was dispatched from Dublin at eight o'clock in the evening and arrived from Cavan at Wattlebridge at ten past five the following morning — passing on via Lisnaskea (not touching Newtownbutler — which was on the Belfast-Enniskillen route) to Enniskillen, which was reached at a quarter to eight. The 'Up' mail was dispatched from Enniskillen at quarter to five and arrived at Wattlebridge at twenty past seven. Dublin was reached at half past four in the morning. These mail coaches conveyed passengers and their luggage.

Upper Lough Erne extends from Wattlebridge to Enniskillen. A steamer plied twice a week between Enniskillen and Belturbet via Wattlebridge to transport goods. From Wattlebridge these goods were conveyed by the Ulster Canal to Portadown and thence to Belfast by railway. The Ulster Canal proceeded from Charlemont, on the Blackwater River and passing south west by Monaghan and Clones it entered Upper Lough Erne at its eastern extremity. Its total length was some forty-eight miles.

A steamer also plied between Lisnaskea and Wattlebridge. Thus it will be seen that a century ago Wattlebridge occupied an important position on the land and water routes which provided transport and communication and served as arteries of trade and traffic.

Those of us who live in an age of air travel, radio and television can never hope to realise what the advent of the mail coach in Wattlebridge meant one hundred years ago.

In the middle of the eighteenth century, a society called 'The Hearts of Steel' was founded in Ulster to aid the farmers in their struggle for tenant rights. Most of its members were Presbyterians, but other religious denominations were well represented.

On the 27 July 1763, about fifty members of 'The Hearts of Steel' from Cavan, Fermanagh and Monaghan assembled at Wattlebridge and were about to proceed to Belturbet Barracks, where they intended to surprise the military and possess themselves of the ammunitions stored there, when they were met by a body of Government troops, led by Charles Coote of Cootehill. The unarmed farmers were defeated with a loss of seven killed fourteen wounded and about thirty prisoners were taken. Only four of the Wattlebridge insurgents, all from the neighbourhood of Scotshouse, were brought to trial. There is no record of the trial. One result of the Ulster Land agitation was the recognition of what is known as the 'Ulster Tenant Right Custom'.

About the year 1870 there was a Post Office at Wattlebridge where the Mail coach delivered and collected the mail. The Post Office then moved to Legakelly about one mile further south, but was set up again at Wattlebridge in the year 1936.

Today, in Wattlebridge, there are several homesteads, one shop, the post office, an Orange Lodge and the ruin of Drumkrin church overlooking the Finn River.

Another feature of Wattlebridge is what is known as the Druid's Temple. This is a most remarkable memorial of primitive man and is situated in Annaghmore townland. The name 'Druid's Temple' is a complete misnomer and dates merely from the opening years of the nineteenth century when the most unusual theories about Irish archaeological and antiquarian remains were in vogue.

The structure on the top of the hill at Wattlebridge is not in any way associated with the Druids, much less with their purely imaginary temples and still more imaginary worship.

Modern scientific research has established beyond doubt that the designation 'Druid's Temple' does not accord with fact and every time this term appears on maps it is entirely misleading. It might be said in its favour that it conveys a faint suggestion of the true origin and purpose of such structures, for all of them are pre-historic burial sites, associated with the actual disposal of the dead or the ritualistic sanctification of the site in question.

The Wattlebridge structure occupies the top of the small hill. It is a circular enclosure, the internal diameter of which is about forty yards. The outer ring of the enclosure is made up of a thorn fence growing through and around a circular row of enormous stone boulders standing close together.

Some of these boulders consist of a hundred cubic feet of stone, if not more and the ring is made up of about eighty gigantic standing stones of this incredible size and weight. The circle is not complete; there is an entrance to the enclosure on the southwestern side of the ring where it touches the track of the ancient road leading from Dublin to Enniskillen.

Within the enclosure itself there is a large stone standing apart on the south eastern side of the enclosure. On the east side of this, lies a flat boulder. Between this standing stone and the outer ring there is a small thicket of bushes growing around three or four large stone boulders. Near this spot was the entrance to an underground chamber but it has been closed up to protect cattle grazing in the enclosure from injury. After a long spell of drought the presence of the underground chamber is indicated by the burnt-up nature of the grass growing over it, whilst the surrounding pasture is green.

This is one of the most impressive works of ancient man in Ireland and its presence affords food for deep thought. The first thing it shows is that a populous and very powerful settlement existed here in remote ages. Just how old it is would be difficult to tell. The oldest megalithic structures date back to the neolithic or late stone age. If we bear in mind that the early Bronze Age of Ireland commenced sometime about 2000 BC we see that the Wattlebridge structure is more than 2000 and it may well be more than 4000 years old.

When we consider that the enormous boulders forming the Wattlebridge structure were not found locally, but had to be transported for miles by water on rafts of timber and then levered up the hill by means of rollers moving on sleepers, we see that large numbers of workmen and a great deal of skill and labour were required for such a gigantic task in a primitive age that lacked the mechanical aids with which modern man is so familiar.

The people who carried out the work must have lived in organised communities and been accustomed to obey the commands of their rulers. They could not have been 'mere savages running wild in the woods' as some writers would have us believe. We are, therefore, brought face to face here with a race of beings of great strength, though we should avoid the error of calling them giants. That they had reached a high degree of civilization and ordered society is abundantly clear.

The so-called 'Druid's Temple' at Wattlebridge is really a megalithic or large stone burial site.

The outer ring of this mighty stone circle is described as a 'cromlech' from two Gaelic words meaning 'curved or circular stones'. The single standing stone is properly called 'Menhir' — a Breton term meaning 'long stone'. The group of unhewn boulders which at one time supported a table stone now fallen, is a 'Dolmen', a compound word derived from Cornish and Breton words meaning 'stone cavity'.

This cavity marked the grave of some great warrior or famous men of old. The outer ring served to set apart and protect the sacred enclosure from desecration. Ancient records would seem to indicate that it was believed that the spirit of the dead warrior entered the stone, which had been erected, to his memory and this belief gave rise to what is known as 'Stone Worship'. The curious belief that stone ate the flesh of the dead prevailed in Egypt and in Greece where a stone coffin was known as a 'sarcophagus' which means flesh eater. This belief about stone 'eating' flesh may have given rise to the idea that the spirit, as well as the flesh of the dead person, entered the stone or stones placed at a tomb.

We have not, unfortunately, any description of this monument prior to the beginning of the eighteenth century when local road makers began to use it as a quarry.

A Mr Nevil, writing from Belturbet in December 1712, says; 'In the county of Fermanagh, on a hill at Wattlebridge there has been a mighty heap of stones. The base is encircled with very large stones. The heap has been removed to make roads and build bridges. During removal, urns were found in stone coffins'.

This so called 'Druid's Temple' at Wattlebridge is frequently visited by learned bodies and may well be thought as worthy of study as other more famous megalithic structures in the British Isles.

seven

Castle Saunderson

Within half a mile of Wattlebridge stands the plantation castle of Castle Saunderson just outside the Fermanagh border in County Cavan. It is situated on a small hill at the eastern end of Upper Lough Erne, in picturesque and wooded surroundings.

The Saundersons came to Ireland from Scotland early in the seventeenth century. The first of them was Alexander Saunderson who received extensive grants of land confiscated from the native Irish. His eldest son, Robert succeeded. He married a Leslie of County Monaghan.

On the 8 January 1689, Robert Saunderson proceeded to Cavan with four score horsemen and dispersed the Justices sitting at the Quarter Sessions that; 'while the laws were unrepealed the writ of Tyrconnell or King James could not run in the country'. By a strange coincidence in County Monaghan at the same time Revd Charles Leslie of Glaslough, was leading the Protestant gentry, who were Williamites, to oppose the Sheriff, appointed by James II as Lord Lieutenant to preside at the sessions in that county.

Robert Saunderson was elected MP for County Cavan in 1692 and again in 1695. In 1696 he was expelled by an order of Parliament because of his political opinions, his place being taken by Francis White of Redhills, County Cavan.

Robert died without issue and the property passed to his nephew, Alexander Saunderson. This man's grandson, another Alexander, married Rose Lloyd. He was a noted gambler and racer. His racecourse may still be seen at Castle Saunderson. He squandered much of the Saunderson property. His son Francis succeeded and by careful management did everything possible to repair the fortunes of the family. He married Anne White, heiress to the Bassett property in Glamorganshire.

Castle Saunderson was twice burned during disturbed times in the seventeenth century.

At the beginning of the eighteenth century Francis Saunderson built the present Castle. He was MP for County Cavan. In the private chapel in the grounds of Castle Saunderson there is a mural tablet to his memory on which there is a Latin inscription outlining many of his fine achievements as 'a good citizen, a faithful friend and an excellent father'.

For the 1783-1790 Parliament, Francis Saunderson was first elected in place of George Montgomery who died whilst representing Cavan County. Francis Saunderson continued to represent Cavan County down to the year 1800.

Castle Saunderson from Wattlebridge, Newtownbutler

Francis was succeeded by his son, Alexander, born 1783. He married the Hon. Sarah Juliana, daughter of the Sixth Baron Farnham of Cavan. He was MP for County Cavan and from 1838 Colonel of the Cavan Militia. In 1846 he left Ireland with his family and lived at Nice until his death in 1857. The callous indifference with which he extracted exorbitant rents from starving tenants during the Famine years, has not endeared his name to posterity.

Colonel Edward Saunderson succeeded. He was Alexander's fourth son, born in 1837. He received his early education at Nice, his tutors being Jesuit priests.

On Alexander's death in 1857 the family returned to England and later settled in Kingstown. Colonel Edward came of age at twenty-five in 1862 and took over the Saunderson property from the Trustees, settling there with his mother and sister Rose.

In 1865, Colonel Edward married Helena de Moleyns, youngest daughter of the Third Lord Ventry, County Kerry. He is chiefly remembered as a yachtsman and politician. All his life he had a passion for designing, building and sailing boats. His spirit should haunt Lough Erne; the chains of his yacht have been placed round his grave. He first entered politics in 1865, being returned unopposed as Liberal MP for County Cavan in place of the Hon. James Maxwell Conservative M.P. who had retired. He was returned unopposed at the next election in 1868. In 1869 he voted against the Bill to disestablish the Church of Ireland, but later confessed that the bill was a blessing owning to the greater freedom enjoyed by the Church of Ireland from Parliamentary control. In the election of 1874 he lost his seat, Mr J. C. Biggar and Mr Fay, both Home Rulers, being returned to represent County Cavan in Parliament.

In 1882 Colonel Edward set out to organise the Orange Lodges.

In 1885 he was returned MP for the constituency of North Armagh. He died 21 October 1906 and is buried 'neath the shadow of a hoary oak in the grounds outside the private chapel'. His statue occupies a commanding site in the town of Portadown.

Colonel Edward had five children, four boys and a girl. He was succeeded by his eldest son, Captain Somerset Saunderson, who married an American, the widow of a German Count and left issue; a twin boy and girl, Alexander and Patricia born in 1918.

Captain Somerset served in the Boar War and in France. During the First World War he was captain of the Rifle Brigade and was later raised to the rank of Major.

When Captain Somerset succeeded his father in 1907 he beautified the estate by having the plantations of Moyhill, Rahulton and Derryhevlin planted. He had a hard tennis court made, also, beside the Castle, which was said to be the second best in Ireland. He introduced a Hornby oil engine for sawing timber for the estate and had his own stonebreaker.

He was interested in yachting, though not to the same extent as his father and he had the famous sailing boat, 'The Witch', remodelled into a house boat.

In 1919 several thousand pounds were spent on renovating the Castle and installing electric light and central heating.

In August 1920 the Castle was raided by Sinn Feiners for ammunition and liquor, during the absence of the Major and his wife. The steward, Mr McCauley, was taken by surprise and made to hand over the keys of the Castle. It was duly raided but no ammunition was found, it having been removed to the Newtownbutler area some days previously.

Shortly after this, the Saundersons left the country and went to live in Berkshire, with the Major's brother, Armour.

Alexander and Patricia were educated in Italy.

In 1921 the Castle was occupied by the Auxiliary Cadets who remained there until the year 1922.

The Saundersons never returned to the Castle. It was left in charge of Mr Hague, Mr Cole and Mr Knight. At this time the Castle went into ruin and much of the timber was sold.

In 1924 the west wing which included; the kitchen and servants' quarters was accidentally burned.

Major Somerset died in England in July 1927. His body was cremated and his ashes placed in the vault of the private chapel at Castle Saunderson.

Captain Alexander succeeded. He was taken prisoner at Dunkirk during the last war. He had been an interpreter at the criminal courts. In 1946 or 1947 he married an American called Midwania. She had been married twice before to two brothers, who were brothers-in-law to Betty Hutton, a well-known actress.

In 1948 Captain Saunderson began the renovation of the Castle. One wing was completed about 1953 and the family moved in. Much more restoration was done in subsequent years. The family led a fairly normal life as large farmers, but had not much connection with the village of Newtownbutler.

Captain Saunderson was chairman of a local band, which is named after his father; 'The Colonel Saunderson Memorial Accordion Band' which is largely composed of musicians from Wattlebridge area.

The Saundersons no longer live at Castle Saunderson but it is possible to view the house on foot via an entrance at a petrol station near the Leggykelly Inn on the Cavan to Clones Road.

Castle Saunderson has unfortunately suffered from fires on various occasions in recent years, but the basic structure remains.

eight

St Comgall's Church of Ireland

The Parish of Galloon is one of the ancient Ecclesiastical establishments of the Diocese of Clogher springing from a monastic settlement on Galloon Island founded by St Tigernach who, before he moved to found the Monastery of Clones, left it in the charge of St Comgall from whom the present Church is named.

The word Galloon like many of the townland names had its origin in the Irish language and is spelt Gabel Luin in the Annals of Ulster, which means 'fork of pool'. A monastery was founded on Galloon Island in the second half of the fifth century. In the years after St Comgall and under a variety of influences the bounds of Galloon's jurisdiction, were extended as it eventually became a parish.

The Parish consisted of land in Fermanagh, which includes the Island townland of Galloon in Upper Lough Erne, in which the parish church stood and also an enormous district in County Monaghan now represented by the parishes of Aghabog, Currin, Drum, Ematris, Killeevan, Newbliss and Rockcorry. The huge extent of this parish is best realised when it is understood that it stretched from the outskirts of Lisnaskea on the west to within a few hundred yards of Cootehill on the east.

Such groups of districts, with resident clergy under the jurisdiction of one Rector and with local chapels, were in the late middle ages known as plebaniae and in the Register of Primate Prene, in 1442, the parish was referred to as the Plebs de Dartraye.

It is frequently referred to in later documents as Galloon alias Dartery. The main parish church ceased to be on Galloon Island in the early part of the seventeenth century as in 1622 it was stated that there was no Rectory and that the church was ruinous. Drumswords Church, now a ruin in Killeevan parish, was the parish church in 1773 and may well have been the same for some time before that date. In the early part of the nineteenth century it was said that no Church existed as such, until in 1823 Newtownbutler Church, which was the Parish Church of Drummully from about 1629, became the Parish Church of Galloon.

This Church in Newtownbutler was burnt in 1641 and was rebuilt in 1648.

It was accidentally burnt in 1819 and rebuilt in 1821 by a grant of £2,000 from the Board of First Fruits.

There is said to have been a church in Newtownbutler before 1629. The building is reputed to have been on the same hill as the present one but slightly to the south. The church has a seating capacity of up to 600 persons and is built in a cruciform shape.

At the west end is a square tower, which tapers to the top, with four storeys and battlements at the corners. A plaque on the outside reads 'North, Clarke and Jo. Robinson Ch. Wks. AD 1814'.

The tower, therefore, predates the rest of the church, which is not surprising, as towers usually are the last section of churches, which fall or are badly damaged in fire or other disasters. Outside the church is a mausoleum where relatives of the Erne family are buried, which dates from the eighteenth century.

Inside, at the west end, is a Georgian gallery supported by cluster-shafted columns, which was built in 1823 according to Select Vestry records of Drummully Parish, as it was then. The first Select Vestry of Galloon in Newtownbutler, which we have a record of, was on the 19 April 1824 with the Revd J. B. Storey as Rector in the chair.

The East Window .... was dedicated, in 1898, by Charles Maurice Stack D.D., former Archdeacon of Clogher, who was appointed Bishop in 1886. He was born at Tubrid, near Kesh in 1825. He returned there in 1902 and lived in Ardess until he died in 1914 (from a book about St Macartan's Cathedral, Clogher). The window is perpendicular in shape and has a conglomeration of small coloured glass pieces set in a geometric design of squares and circles giving a pleasing effect. It was badly damaged by the big bomb of 1974 but was expertly restored.

The South Window .... is dedicated to the memory of Robin Bell, Robin Forde, Victor Morrow, Richard Latimer and Robert Crilly who were murdered by terrorists. The window incorporates the badges of the U.D.R. and the RUC who both subscribed substantial sums.

On Remembrance Sunday a Poppy wreath is placed on The First World War Memorial Plaque which commemorates those who gave their lives for King and Country; Lord Crichton, B. Parkinson-Cumine, Joseph Armstrong, M. McGirr, Wm. Woods and James Doonan. Two wreaths are also laid at the memorial window in memory of the RUC and U.D.R. victims already mentioned.

The Church was re-seated in 1889 and the flagged floor replaced by tiles during the 1960s.

The ceilings have plaster work of outstanding beauty which were reported to have been done by craftsmen from Italy when they were commissioned to do the plaster at Crom Castle about the time that the Castle was being rebuilt. At the corner of the transepts there are medallions and around the cornice are lilies, acorns, vines, oak leaves and dishes of fruit. The circular decoration over the crossing has a solid circular surround enclosing a border of vines and in the centre are flowers and acanthus leaves in a whirl. The West transept ceiling has a small circle where the pipe of the old heater emerged, as well as another rosette with twelve points with ivy and rose-like flowers surrounding the acanthus swirl of leaves in the centre. The east ceiling, about the choir stalls is a decoration similar to the west ceiling but having sixteen points. At a first glance the north transept ceiling looks rather like the south transept ceiling but on further investigation the one in the north side has cornets of fruit, the one on the south side has no cornets.

Certainly the plants used have some reference to either the Bible of mythology. The oak is rich in mystic associations and rooted deeply in our folklore. The lily is associated with The Madonna and the vine with Christ.

There are several monuments in the church, one to William West of Drumralla who died in 1897 aged seventy-one and his wife, Margaret West and two sons, The Revd James Joseph West who died in 1900 aged thirty-three years and Thomas West who died in 1904 aged forty-eight. It was erected by a daughter, Elizabeth Armstrong.

Another is to Fanny, wife of Revd Alex E. Auchinleck and daughter of John Crozier of Gortra House, Esq. J.P. Age thirty-six erected by her husband.

A third is to the family of Robinson, which reads .... Wm. Robinson of Feaugh House, died 1911 aged forty-seven and wife Helen Charlotte, died 1923 aged fifty-nine and daughter Phyllis Kathleen died 1920, aged seventeen years.

The Church of Ireland, Newtownbutler

There is a small plaque to Francis Creighton Fitzgerald L.R.P.C.I. L.R.C.S.I. died 1936 in his eighty-eighth year.

The font stands on a square plinth with octagonal stem. The basin is also octagonal with a wooden lid with wrought iron trimming. It is made of cut sandstone.

The oldest silver has Drummully Parish Church inscribed on it dated 1776. These items include an alms dish, a flagon, a chalice and a paten.

The lights originally hung from metal circles, which were in keeping with the decor of the time. New lights were installed about 1960 and these were replaced in 1992 in memory of the late Albert Elliott of Crom Lane.

There was a pipe organ at the beginning of the century. It was replaced by a Harmonium and this was replaced by an electronic organ, which in its turn was followed by the present one in 1983. In the past teachers at the school were expected to play the organ. Some of the organists were Miss Beatie, Miss McCarrison, Mr R. H. Harris, Mr G. B. Mitchell, Mrs Mount, Miss Greta Crowe, Mrs W. Boles, Miss Doreen Moore, Miss Sandra Barnard, Revd J. Montgomery, Miss Laura Bell, Miss Hilary Bell, Miss Jean Hetherington, Miss Christine Kerr, and Mrs Edie Johnston.

Within living memory, the Sextons were Mr Robert Alien of Drumquilla, Mr Robert Moncrieff of Main Street, and Mr Sandy Moncrieff of Drumclay. Mr William Phair of Treacy Terrace was the next Sexton and he is ably assisted by his wife, Maisie.

List of Rectors

1409 Revd Henry Macconly McMahon
1409 Revd Eneas O'Carbi
1424 Revd Charles McAdam
1427 Revd Malachy O'Bruyn
1428 Revd Charles McAdam
1428 Revd James McMahon
1440 Revd John O'Sheehy
1441 Revd Magonius O'Connolly
1448 Revd Arthur McCraith
1483 Revd Eneas O'Karlbrey
1486 Revd Philip McMahon
1492 Revd Thomas McMahon
1529 Revd Matthew O'Conaly
1532 Revd Arthur O'Murchay
1532 Revd Patrick Maccurta
1533 Revd Magonius McVallum
1617 Revd Edward Hatton
1624 Revd George Mackeson
1631 Revd James Hatton
1637 Revd Archibald Erskine
1637 Revd James Margetson
1658 Revd Patrick Kerr
1663 Revd Michael Boyle
1678 Revd John Parker
1679 Revd George Lovell
1681 Revd John Forster
1705 Revd Dillon Ashe
1716 Revd Arthur St George
1773 Revd Thomas Campbell
1795 Revd Andrew Allen
1804 Revd John Benjamin Story
1844 Revd Henry Tottenham
1847 Revd John Richardson
1866 Revd John Crozier Hudson
1876 Revd Abraham Jagoe
1884 Revd George Gardiner Parkinson-Cumine
1916 Revd James Condell Taylor
1941 Revd Thomas Stothers
1951 Revd Nevil O'Neill
1981 Revd John Hay
1989 Revd Nigel Peter Baylor
1995 Revd Alan Synott
2001 Revd Brian Crowe
2003 Revd David Luckman
2005 now vacant

nine

The Rectory

The Old Rectory was in the house now occupied by the Northern Bank. The last Rector to live there was Canon Parkinson-Cumine, who was the first incumbent to occupy the Rectory on Crom Road. The last family who lived in the Old Rectory on the High Street was a family of Bells who later moved to Sheeney.

The land on which the present Rector stands, belonged to the Earl of Lanesborough and this was purchased from him and the agreement was settled on behalf of the Parish by the Diocesan Trustees who were; The Right Reverend Maurice Day D.D. Bishop of Clogher, The Right Hon. John Henry Crichton Earl of Erne, The Hon. Armar Lowry Corry and Hugh De Fellenburg Montgomery.

The plans for the Rectory were drawn up by W. R. Potts of Green-bank, Clones on 23 April 1913. The Contractor was Joseph McMahon Junior, of Newtownbutler Road, Clones, who originally agreed to build the house and outhouses for the sum of nine hundred and eighty two pounds sterling. The Rector is fortunate to have in his possession the original plans and specifications for the Rectory as well as the original contract which was obtained from Mr George Knight of Clones, whose forebear, M. E. Knight, was the Diocesan Solicitor of the day.

The Butlers have been connected with the neighbourhood for over 300 years and by a curious coincidence, the Rectory now occupies the site of an old Castle of the Butlers built in the seventeenth century. Mrs Sam McCoy has given some interesting information as to the laying of the foundation stone of the Rectory. The foundation stone was laid on Easter Eve, April 1914, by the Earl of Lanesborough. A large number of parishioners assembled to take part in the proceedings and an address was given by the Lord Bishop of Clogher, the Right Reverend Maurice Day.

One particularly novel method of raising money for the building of the Rectory was the compilation of a book of quotations by Mrs Louise A. Johnston and Miss Catherine C. Walker. They charged 2 shillings and sixpence for each quotation submitted and printed along with the person's name. People from throughout Fermanagh and Monaghan and the rest of Ireland submitted quotations and the book raised £200, a considerable sum in those days. First printed in 1913, this book of quotations has been reprinted in exactly the same form by the original printers. A picture of the Rectory has been added with a preface from the present Bishop and

The Rectory

with a list of all the incumbents who have occupied the Rectory since it was built.

Copies of this book are available from Mrs Joan Allen and Miss Margery Armstrong of 8 Bridge Street, Newtownbutler, both daughters of the compilers; Miss Catherine C. Walker.

The Rectory was originally supplied with water from a well within the grounds at the upper left-hand corner, until it was connected to the mains supply during the 1950s.

The Rectory was extensively renovated towards the end of Canon O'Neill's incumbency and further improved by the installation of a central heating system at the beginning of Revd Hay's tenure in office.

The Revd Hay was also responsible for transforming the Rectory grounds with the help of many of the parishioners.

Another significant event was a tree-planting ceremony, which took place in March 1987. Each family was invited to purchase a tree of their own choice for an allocated site, which was on a numbered chart. The trees were supplied by Baronscourt Nursery, whose representative, Mr David Wilson, was present to assist with the planting.

Her Grace the late Dowager Duchess of Abercorn, who was a sister of the 5th Lord Erne and who herself was brought up at Crom and the present Lord and Lady Erne were also at the tree planting.

The Rectory has also been able to benefit in many ways from the generosity of parishioners, such as front gates, the resurfacing of the back courtyard and other gifts.

ten

Sallaghy Parish

This Parish is situated mainly in the area between Newtownbutler and Lisnaskea and the church itself is on the old road. It was formed out of Galloon, Newtownbutler in the year 1840. The foundation stone of the Church was laid by Mrs Selina G. Crichton who, with her husband, Lt-Col. John Crichton, came from Crom Castle. The Act of Dedication was conducted by the Venerable Archdeacon Russell of the Clogher Diocese on 13 July.

Included in the large congregation was the Revd John M. Graydon, Curate of Galloon, who, presumably, was in charge of the Parish until it became a separate entity. The Church was consecrated on the 4 July 1843.

A Service in connection with the Centenary was held on Saturday 13 July 1940 at 3.30 pm when the preacher was the Very Reverend W. S. Kerr, B.D., then Dean of Belfast and later Bishop of Down, Connor and Dromore. The Clergyman in charge of the Parish was the Reverend George S. Hogg, B.A., later Archdeacon of Cashel, who now resides in retirement in Tramore, County Waterford.

The 150th Anniversary of the formation of the Parish was being celebrated on the 14 July 1990 at a special service in Sallaghy Church. Former Clergy of the Parish were present and the Bishop of Clogher, the Rt. Revd B. D. A. Hannon, M.A., gave the Address on this historic occasion.

To celebrate the 150th Anniversary a new Church Hall was built in 1991 adjacent to the Church, much to the credit of the Rector and parishioners.

Sallaghy Church of Ireland 2005

eleven

St Mary's Roman Catholic Church

The Roman Catholic Church of the Immaculate Conception has a common history with the local Church of Ireland Parish of Galloon in that both originate from the Monastery founded by St Tighernach early in the sixth century on Galloon Island. That early common history has been outlined elsewhere but the actual separation seems to have come at the end of the sixteenth and the beginning of the seventeenth century. This was the period of the conquest of Ireland by colonisation when many of the local clergy would have been replaced by clergy of the Established Church.

The result of this was that many of the priests of the Roman Catholic Church had to operate under different circumstances. They had to move around in disguise and risked being betrayed by those looking for a reward of one kind or another. Lists of priests were drawn up by the authorities but these were subsequently burnt during the bombing of the Public Records Office in the Four Courts in Dublin during the Civil War, which followed British withdrawal from the twenty-six counties of Ireland. That is why the list of priests which is found at the end of this account is incomplete and we are dependant on research done by Tony Murphy in a parish history written in the late 1980s. In 1704 the parishes of Galloon and Drummully were united under Revd Philip McIlgunn. This is interesting because the Church of Ireland parishes of Galloon and Drummully have had links since this period also and the Church in Newtownbutler was Drummully Parish Church from 1629 until 1823. The parishes were separated at a later period in time.

The location of a chapel in Newtownbutler in the years following is difficult to be certain about, but the earliest site is said to have been a mud-wall building thatched with straw, during Revd Francis Goodwin's time in Newtownbutler. John McDonnell of Derrydoon told Francis Fitzpatrick in 1923 that his mother Betty Fitzpatrick of Derrykenny went with her mother to Mass in it and she gave her son a good description of it. It was located alongside the river where the curate's house was, in Main Street. Patrick Murray, who died in March 1914, aged 113 years, is reported to have said that in his youth he had assisted at Mass in an old thatched Church on that site.

The present Church was built about 1821 during the pastorate of the Revd Francis Goodwin. A bell-tower was erected while Revd Patrick Traynor was Administrator in the absence of

The Roman Catholic Chapel

the Revd James Clarke. The Church was in a dilapidated condition when Canon O'Connor undertook its renovation in 1896. A small piece of land beside the Church was purchased from the Earl of Lanesborough for an extension to the Church.

Canon O'Connor's name appears on the stained glass altar window. The window depicts the Crucifixion and is even more beautiful when the setting sun shines through it.

It was about 1906 that the spire was added and at the top holding the cross was a beautiful golden orb, which shone for miles around in good weather. One of the most treasured possessions of the parish is what is known as the 'Donegan Chalice'. This was donated to Father Clarke in 1860 by John Donegan, a Jeweller in Dublin, originally from Newtownbutler.

The Graveyard was renovated and extended during the 1930s and the priest's graves were moved from the north east side to their new resting-place in the new graveyard. At that time some top soil from the graveyard was removed and ended up at Lurganboy House. The Chapmans recall Canon Maguire saying that he would be glad to be buried in their garden as it was holy ground in his estimation.

The original gateway was farther down the hill nearly opposite the back gate of Lurganboy House.

During this renovation the beautiful orb disappeared.

The sandstone used in the building and the outside decorations over the windows came from the Eshbrally Quarry between Lisnaskea and Ballagh.

The Church was renovated again in 1987 when it was reseated and carpeted. The marble altar was removed and replaced by a table so the Priest could face the congregation.

In the graveyard is a tombstone erected to Sarah Crudden who was the Foundress of St Joseph's Orphanage in Bundoran. She died in 1899.

Another well-known name amongst the congregation is Father Ignatius McQuillan who became the President of St Columb's College in Londonderry, having been ordained in June 1955.

Thirty-six years later Father Gary Donegan, in June 1991, was ordained and celebrated his first Mass at St Mary's, Newtownbutler. He joined the Passionists' school retreat and missionary team.

The Revd Jimmy McPhillips, also of Newtownbutler, studied for the priesthood and was ordained in 1992.

In years past, both the Parish Priest and the Curate lived in two houses on Main Street next to the Orange Hall. About twenty years ago a bungalow was built for the Parish Priest near Gould's Ring in Drumquillia and in 1990 the Curate had a house built on a slightly lower level from the bungalow.

It is curious to note that the Curate now lives in a larger residence than the Parish Priest Maybe it's a sign of the times.

Organists in recent years; Miss Ginny Loyld (Clones) deceased, Miss Veronica Cadden, Mrs Mai McAvinney, Miss Loraine West and Miss Fiona Wilson.

List of Parish Priests

1651 Revd T. Connolly

1671 Fr Philip Beggan

1704 Revd Philip McIlgunn was P.P. when Galloon and Drummully were united.

1731 Revd McMahon

1757 Revd Felix Mulligan

   Revd Bernard Casey died 1799

1800 Revd Francis Goodwin who said Mass at the Mud Chapel

1837 Revd J. Clarke

1857 Revd Patrick Traynor (Administrator) to 1862

   Revd James Clarke Died 1876

   Revd Hugh Ward

   Canon Daniel O'Connor (His name is on the altar window)

   Revd Philip McGinnity died 1914

   Revd Thomas O'Doherty

1936 - 1954 Canon Maguire resigned after eighteen years

1960 - 1965 Revd Henry O'Hanlon who had previously been Administrator for six years

1965 - 1983 Canon Duffy

1983 Canon E. Murphy

1988 Father Michael King

twelve

The Methodist Church in Newtownbutler

We are very indebted to Revd Dudley Cooney, who left the area in 1990, for the information following which was taken from his very comprehensive history of the Methodist Church in these parts.

A copy of this can be obtained from the Library in Enniskillen.

The Methodist Church owes its origins to the Revd John Wesley in the mid-eighteenth century. John Wesley visited Ireland in 1756 and he paid his first visit to Fermanagh in 1762. Although John Wesley himself does not seem to have visited Newtownbutler, one of his itinerant preachers Mr John Smith does seem to have come to the village towards the end of 1766. In 1777 John Clarke of Cortrasna opened a shop, presumably in Newtownbutler and travelling Methodist preachers are known to have stayed in the house.

In 1790 it was decided to build a chapel, which is thought to have been located somewhere on Main Street. By 1812 many Methodists were agitating for the administration of the sacrament of Holy Communion in the chapels, but it was argued that such an act would be tantamount to separation from the Established Church in Ireland. In 1818 the Primitive Wesleyan Society was established. This Society maintained its contact with the Church of Ireland by continuing to receive the sacrament of Holy Communion in the Parish Church. Mr William Thompson, born at Cornabrass, Newtownbutler, was elected to succeed John Wesley as the President of the British Conference of the Methodists. The house where he was born still stands at Cornabrass on land owned by Mr Walter Liddle.

The Wesleyan Church as we know it today on the High Street was built in 1835. Henry Taylor, the Secretary and General Missionary of the Primitive Wesleyan Conference, visited Newtownbutler in 1849 and a service is held each year at Feaugh on the first Sunday in July to commemorate this.

In 1858 the Primitive Wesleyans developed a Society at Drumady and a service is still held there each Sunday afternoon. In 1870 the disestablishment of the Church of Ireland presented problems for Methodism. Throughout their years of separate existence the Methodists had attended the Church of Ireland for sacraments, marriages and funerals. From this time onwards Methodists began slowly to administer these rites within their own churches.

The building now known as the Orange Hall was once a Methodist Church and those who called themselves Methodists met there, while the Primitive Wesleyans met in the Church on High Street already mentioned.

The Methodist Church

In 1878 the two churches amalgamated and the Church on High Street was used. In 1921, owing to political and commercial circumstances and the formation of the Border, there was an exodus of Protestants from the area and membership in the Church diminished. In 1965, the Irish Methodist Revival Movement was formed, of which Mr Jack Morton of Newtownbutler was secretary. Eventually, this led to the formation of the Free Methodist Church.

The Methodist Church on High Street suffered bomb damage from IRA attacks on the RUC Station next door in 1974 and 1989. The Methodist Manse actually had to be relocated from Newtownbutler to Lisnaskea in the late 1980s when the RUC wanted to extend the boundaries of its Station.

A house on High Street now occupied by Nurse McLoughlin used to be the Methodist Manse in former days. One of the Methodist Ministers who occupied this Manse was Revd Mr Conlin who was the grandfather of the late Miss Molly Johnston, also of High Street.

The Methodist Church celebrated its 150th Anniversary in 1985.

A list of Methodist Ministers since 1902

1902 Revd Albert G. Glanville
1905 Revd Robert Maxwell
1908 Revd Samuel G. McIntyre
1911 Revd John Coulter
1912 Revd Samuel G. McIntyre
1913 Revd James Gibson
1916 Revd John J. Hutchinson
1919 Revd John Sanderson
1922 Revd William J. Rooney
1925 Revd William J. Young
1927 Revd James Johnston
930 Revd Frederick McIvoe
1934 Revd William Bryans
1939 Revd John Montgomery
1944 Revd Robert A. Knowles
1947 Revd Thomas Hartley
1952 Revd A. H. Boyd
1957 Revd D. Wesley Morrow
1961 Revd Robert A. Parkhill
1966 Revd W. Graham Hamilton
1971 Revd Derek Russell
1976 Revd Paul Kingston
1982 Revd D. A. L. Cooney
1990 Revd Christopher Walpole
1996 Revd Andrew Kingston
1996 Mrs Eleanor Haydon (Lay Assistant)
2001 Revd Paul Ritchie
2004 Revd Michael Gregory

thirteen

The Presbyterian Church

Presbyterianism in Newtownbutler began in the 1920s when the Border was established. Monthly services were held in the old market house (now the Church Hall), but when permission was refused to hold fortnightly services, the Presbyterian Church in the Crom Road was built at a total cost of £150. The opening service was held on 26 July 1937. The preacher was the then Moderator of the General Assembly, Dr John Waddell.

The minister's room was built on to the church building in 1960 and in 1963 the car park was acquired. In 1986 extensive repairs were made to the windows, floor and wiring.

Some members shared in the inter-church fellowship for prayer and bible study in The Rectory. Brian McConkey was one of the Congregation and is at present an evangelist with Cliff College, Derbyshire (1987).

A pulpit, bible and communion table were presented, at the 50th Anniversary Service on Sunday, 26 July 1987, in memory of Mr T. J. Anderson who died in 1986 after many years of faithful service as session clerk. He had been involved in every aspect of the Church's life and had much to do with the construction in 1937.

In the early days it was regarded as a mission church or mission station, but in 1966 Newtownbutler and Lisnaskea became separate congregations sharing a minister with Maguiresbridge and Lisbellaw.

At the 50th Anniversary Service, Miss Isobel Anderson was the Organist and Miss Carol Somerville was the Soloist.

Ministers

Revd J. I. Stoops was the first pastor	Revd Kirkwood 1991
Revd W. T. Agnew began weekly services in 1941	Revd Geoffrey Allen 1998
Revd C. R. J. Brown (1951-1955)	
Revd E. T. Conn (1956-65)	
Revd K. Gregg (1967-1978)	
Revd J. G. Faris (1981-1988)	

The Presbyterian Church

fourteen

Parish of Drummully

Drummully Parish is included in the 'Story of Newtownbutler' because of its old church connections with the village.

The patron saint of the parish of Drummully is Saint Coman.

The benefice is referred to in fifteenth century papal documents as St Comma's of Drummaelchi. It is not mentioned in the Ecclesiastical Taxation of 1306, so it was probably then included in some other parish. The first Vicar appears to have been Donatus O'Goan, elsewhere referred to as John O'Gowan, who held office up to the year 1428. The original Parish Church stood on the townland of Drummully.

The only record we have of the original boundaries of the parish comes from a document known as the Inquisition of the 7th James I.

This document written in the beginning of the seventeenth century stated that the parish embraced 'six balibetaghes and two tales of the new measure' (5,880 acres). This consisted of 'Ballindrumloan, Ballyletureyne, Ballinchulin and three-quarters of Comyna, lying on the half barony of Cuynanar and also Ballyrenvillie, Ballinchirrin, Tonaghboy and the quarter of Carrowgarcragh, lying in Clandelly'.

The parsonage or Rectory seems to have been under the control of the Abbot of Clones and a Vicar was appointed to the parish. The tithes were paid in kind with the local Lord or herenach paying two thirds and the clergy one third. There was a Chapel of Ease at Donaghmoyline with half a tate of land attached. (This probably refers to Donagh). The spellings of many parishes and townlands have obviously changed over the centuries but it is interesting to note the earlier names, which were used. Drummully itself comes from the Irish meaning 'the ridge of the summit'.

As in every other parish in the diocese, the Church and its property here were handed over to the Protestant Settlers at the time of confiscation at the beginning of the seventeenth century. In 1622, an Ecclesiastical Report stated that the Church was in ruins and that no glebe house existed.

The Church is marked in the Baronial Maps of 1609-1610 as if it was then intact. We can only speculate as to what happened to the Church in the intervening ten years. The parish church was not rebuilt on its original site but in 1629 another church was built and a churchyard laid out in Newtownbutler, within the parish boundaries and was already in use. It was decided in that year that this Church should become the Parish Church of Drummully and so it and its

The Church of Ireland, Drummully, Newtownbutler

successors remained until 1823. When Drumkrin was formed as a parish in 1773 Drummully actually lost the site of its ancient Parish Church. However, in 1804, when Drumkrin was dissolved, the ancient church site returned to Drummully. Drummully did, however, lose the north western part of the parish to Galloon, which included its parish church in Newtownbutler. In the Diocesan reorganisation of parish boundaries, Drummully did gain that part of Drumkrin, which contained the parish church of St Mary's, Drumkrin. For a period of time up to 1844, when the present Church of Drummully was built, the church at Drumkrin was used as the parish church. The new Church was named St Mary's, it would seem after St Mary's, Drumkrin and the original St Coman was dropped as the patron saint.

One interesting entry in the burial records of Drummully shows a John Moore of Clonkee who was buried on 6 May 1916 at the age of ninety-six years and a note shows that he was a Sunday school teacher in St Mary's, Drumkrin, prior to 1844.

In the Roman Catholic Church organisaton of parishes during the seventeenth and eighteenth centuries, the Parish Priest of Drummully administered Galloon and visa versa. It is interesting that this close relationship mirrors the Church of Ireland situation down the centuries. In fact when Father Francis Goodwin P.P. took up residence in Newtownbutler around 1800, the parish of Galloon and Drummully became known as Drummully. The Donegan chalice mentioned earlier has inscribed on it that it was 'Presented to the Parish of Drummully by John Donegan, 20 December 1848, Revd J. Clarke P.P.'

In 1955 Bishop O'Callagh decided to revert to the older form of parochial names. As a result Newtownbutler became known as Galloon and the parish of Currin became known as Drummully.

Philip Moore of Newtownbutler Road, Clones, has written a fuller history of Currin parish in his book 'The Story of the G.A.A. in Currin and an Outline of Parish History' and readers would benefit from this in getting a more complete picture. In 1980 the Conons area of Currin parish was incorporated into Clones Parish and the two townlands of Kiltober and Clonkee were incorporated into the Parish of Galloon. At this point in time the title of the Parish of Drummully only applies to the small Church of Ireland Parish which is situated in County Monaghan, in the barony of Dartry and partly in County Fermanagh, in the baronies of Clonkelly and Coole about four miles respectively from Clones and Belturbet.

During this century the Church of Ireland parish of Drummully was joined at different times to Clones Parish and Scotshouse Parish. However, in 1962, Drummully became amalgamated with Galloon Parish under the rectorship of the Revd Nevil O'Neill. A finely built school stood beside the Church for many years at which many of the Drummully parishioners attended until the late fifties when it closed. The Union Hall and another smaller hall were situated at some distance from the Church on the road to Clones. Only the smaller hall remains intact today. Both of these buildings were used for social and religious events in the parish down the years. Drummully School eventually took over as the parochial hall up until the mid-1980s.

Unfortunately, it was burnt at this point in time and a new hall was built on the site, which serves the small congregation to this day. This small parish still maintains its unique witness as a cross-border Church of Ireland congregation which is proud of its rich heritage. It has as one of its former members the present Bishop of Repton in the Church of England, the Right Reverend Henry Richmond, whose family still worship in the Church.

Clergymen of Drummully

Vicars

1428	Revd Donagus O'Gowan
1428	Revd Tatheus O'Gowan
1429	Revd Eugene O'Connolly
1432	Revd Malachi O'Gowan
1436	Revd Thady O'Gowan
1448	Revd Thomas MacGillacoyaghy
1619	Revd Geoffrey Middleton (who was first Headmaster of Fermanagh Royal School in 1618)
1622	Revd John Gregg (who resided in Trim, County Meath)

Rectors and Vicars (Church of Ireland)

1625	Revd Richard Hachett
1627	Revd Richard Morse
1638	Revd John Heygate
1640	Revd Edward Synge (later Bishop of Cork, Cloyne and Ross (1663))
1661	Revd Alexander Keith
1670	Revd John Leslie
1672	Revd Alexander Semple

1675	Revd John Leslie (returned)
1721	Revd Samuel Madden
1766	Revd John Maxwell
1784	Revd William Major
1792	Revd James Hastings
1823	Revd Hon. John Pratt Hewitt
1828	Revd Francis Gervais
1849	Revd Joseph Galwell
1853	Revd Valentine Duke Christian
1872	Revd Thomas Richard Conway
1908	Revd W. B. Stack
1910	Revd James Condell Taylor
1916	Revd John Robert Meara
1926	Revd Benjamin Northridge
1931	Revd E. A. Forster
1943	Revd R. A. Robinson (Curate in charge)
1944	Revd W. W. Nash (Curate in charge)
1951	Revd J. A. M. McNutt
1956	Revd R. J. Williamson
1961	Revd Nevil O'Neill
1981	Revd John Hay
1989	Revd Nigel Baylor

Roman Catholic Priests

From 1704 when Galloon and Drummully were united, the list is the same as is found in the notes on St Mary's, Newtownbutler.

The Church of St Mary's, Drumkrin

This Church, of which only the tower now remains, is situated on the Wattlebridge Road leading to Cavan before one reaches the Cavan-Clones Road.

Drumkrin ('the ridge of the tree') was formed as a parish in 1773 from certain townlands taken from the parishes of Galloon and Drummully.

It is interesting to note some of the townlands, which made up this parish of Drumkrin; Gubdoah, Goladuff, Drummully, Cloncorick, Cloncallick, Mullanalack, Gubadilla, Hermitage, Lisnaderk, Derrykerrib, Gubb and Killanibber in the island of Galloon. The parish of Drumkrin had a short history as it was dissolved on 17 January 1804.

One portion of Drumkrin was united to Currin and the other to Drummully while Galloon received the island of Galloon back within its parochial boundaries again. The late Colonel Saunderson used to tell that once he worshipped at morning service in Drumkrin Church with his mother, who in consequence of the state of the roof had to open her umbrella during the service to protect them from the passing shower.

After 1841, Drumkrin Church became the parish church of Drummully until the new Church was built in 1844 on the Cavan-Clones Road. The original Church of St Mary's was to be built in Kilgarrow but was built instead in Drumkrin. The first Rector of St Mary's was

The ruin of the old Church at Drumquin, Newtownbutler 2005

Revd Thomas Campbell who was a distinguished academic receiving the degrees of L.L.B. and L.L.D. in 1772 from Trinity College, Dublin and who had several publications to his name on history, philosophy and politics.

The last Rector was Revd William Moffatt who was appointed Rector of Currin in 1804 but who held that part of Drumkrin, which was to go to Drummully until 1841 when he died.

The Rectory for Drumkrin was at Parson's Green where Revd William Moffatt lived until he retired. It is interesting to note that when the parish of Drumkrin was in existence, it contained not only the original site of the parish church of Galloon on Galloon Island but also the site of the pre-reformation Parish Church of Drummully.

The history of the Church of Ireland parishes of Galloon, Drumkrin and Drummully are therefore interwoven like a celtic design. The old silver plate in St Mary's, Drummully, has 'Drumkrin' inscribed on it and the chalice; paten and flagon used regularly in Drummully at Holy Communion Services are constant reminders of Drumkrin's former history.

fifteen

The Church Hall/Market House

The Church Hall, as it is now called, was originally 'The Market House', which was designed by W. D. Butler of Dublin. The Earl of Lanesborough commissioned Mr Philip Reilly to build The Market House in 1830. The Contractor, who was from Derrylin, was the grandfather of Dr Cormac Reilly and the great-grandfather of Mr Dermot McCormack. He also built the Lanesborough Arms Hotel, next to The Market House. (The Hotel is locally known as Reilly's).

Markets were held each Friday and fairs for yarn and butter were held on the second Friday of each month.

In 1919 the Revd J. C. Taylor, the Church of Ireland Rector (grandfather of Mrs Tilson of Drummully Post Office), purchased the Hall for his parishioners.
The first floor, known as the Parochial Hall, was used by the parishioners for various activities, while the Thompson Brothers used the ground floor of the building for their egg business from the 1920s. Thompsons sent lorries to collect eggs from farmers over a wide area and brought them back to the Hall were they were tested and packed. In the early days the testers 'candled' the eggs by holding them in front of a candle flame to check that they were perfect before packing.

Travelling grocery salesmen bought eggs also from the farmers and these they sold to Thompsons. The farmers' wives bought their groceries and meal with the egg money. Mrs D. F. Clarke of Enniskillen was at that time a poultry instructress who travelled round the county giving advice.

In the 1930s eggs were bought for a shilling (5p) per dozen. Now in 1990 they are around 80p (100p to the pound sterling). The eggs were exported to England and Scotland.
Church records also show that in 1920 the Church leased the ground floor to Mr McCormack for £10 per month for the purpose of trading in eggs and butter. Butter was tested in various ways and some even dipped their finger in to test the quality and flavour!

Before the Presbyterian Church was built the Presbyterians used the first floor for their services. The first floor of the Hall was also used as a temporary classroom when in 1943 and oak tree fell on the old school building.

During the Second World War, a canteen was held in the Hall for members of the Armed Services... The Seaforth Highlanders, The Berkshires and members of the United States Army and Airforce who were billeted at Crom. The little kitchen at the top of the stone stairs was

This is the Churches Hall (Church of Ireland, Methodist and Presbyterian)

where the cooking was done on an old fashioned solid-fuel range. The food was served on a counter in the Hall.

In 1971 the Church Vestry asked Mr Robert Robinson to repair the building and make it suitable for a Church Hall. A committee was formed and money was raised by organising dances, dinners, barbecues, firework displays, etc.

The work commenced early in 1971 and was finished by August of the same year at a cost of £10,000.

The joists of the original building were of valuable pitch pine, in perfect condition. These were used for the ground floor, as an upstairs room was not needed. Hence the ceiling of the Hall was raised.

The upstairs windows were retained in order to keep the original outside facade of the building. A twisted stone staircase had led to the first storey. This was removed, step by step, by Mr Ronald Johnston.

The back of the Hall now contains a committee room, kitchen and toilets.

All the building materials for the Hall were obtained at cost price, mostly from J. W. H. Johnston, the hardware merchant in Newtownbutler.

The Hall was officially opened by The Rt. Hon. Earl of Erne on Wednesday, 18 November 1971. A photograph of the opening shows... Revd K. Gregg, Mr Jack Leahy, The Earl of Erne,

Revd N. O'Neill, Mr R. Robinson, Revd G. Hamilton, Mrs Armstrong, Mrs Gregg, Mrs Hamilton and Mr J. C. Burke.

On the wall of the Hall is a framed tablecloth. Mrs Jack Armstrong raised £260 by embroidering on the cloth the name of each person who contributed money.

The Hall is now used for cubs, brownies, guides, bowls, badminton and other church functions.

It is maintained by the Church of Ireland, the Methodists and the Presbyterians and is run by a joint Committee of the same.

A new hall has been created at the back of the main hall out of two former sheds. A rear exit has also been made which leads onto Crom Lane and thanks are due to Mrs S. Johnston and Mr D. McCormack for legal permission to aid this particular development. A new staircase has also been put in, leading to another new room upstairs for recreational use.

This work was done largely by Mr Alan McCartney, who gave of his many gifts to see this project completed and to whom the three churches are extremely grateful. This development was dedicated by Revd Nevil O'Neill on the evening of 27 September 1991, at 8.00 p.m. and was named the Trinity Hall.

sixteen

The Community Centre (Court House)

The building stands at the southwest corner of the crossroads in the middle of the town. The building is in the form of a 'T' with a large hall occupying the central part. Inside the building, the floor in the hall was level in the centre and rose in tiers for the court. There was a witness box on one side and the dock was on the north side next to where the Fordes now live. Mrs Forde's pantry was the prison cell. On the wall opposite the main entrance was a balcony for the judge's seat and the door behind it led into a retiring room for the judge. While on circuit the Judge was a guest of J. W. Johnston of Main Street. Petty Sessions were held on the second Wednesday of each month.

Once a year, the local shop-keepers had to take their Imperial Weights and Measures to the Court House to be tested so that members of the public were not sold the wrong quantities of goods in the shops.

At this time, goods were packaged in the local shops by the shop assistants. They were not factory packed as they are today. The original weights and measures are kept in the Enniskillen Museum and were on view at the 'Crafted in Fermanagh' Exhibition during March 1988. A mark was put on the weights when checked.

In the 1920s the building was used by a security force known as the 'A' Specials. Major Parkinson-Cumine, a son of the Rector, was in charge.

Later (about 1930 onwards) badminton was played in the hall and sales of work were held there also. During the Second World War it was used by the Ministry of Defence to billet troops while other accommodation was prepared for them. Dances were held there to entertain the troops. While the Courts were in progress these activities were in abeyance.

During the Troubles the frontage was damaged by a bomb. This was later repaired by a less artistic structure of brick. After this the building was protected by a large wire fence and steel barrels filled with cement. These were taken away in 1987.

In 1988 the hall was in fact purchased by the Fermanagh District Council from the Northern Ireland Court's Service and renamed the Community Centre. Since then it has been used for a variety of activities including whist drives, upholstery classes and the Thursday club for senior citizens.

It therefore serves the whole community in Newtownbutler and is a venue at which everyone feels comfortable.

Newtownbutler, Court House

seventeen

Education in the Newtownbutler Area

At the end of the 1700s and the beginning of the 1800s, the school system was not what it is today. Most of the teaching was done by itinerant teachers who set up a school wherever there was a need. These schools were known as hedge schools. A hedge school was not necessarily under a hedge, but perhaps in a building with a valuation of less than £5. The salary of the teacher was brought to school by the pupils at the rate of a penny per week. A teacher's wage was about £11 per year, roughly equivalent to that of a labourer. In 1826 there were fourteen schools in the Parish of Galloon; many of these were hedge schools.

Alongside these schools were schools sponsored by societies such as the London Hibernian Society and the Kildare Place Society. There is record of a school, receiving a grant from the Kildare Place Society, being established in Newtownbutler in 1825. The first master was a Mr Morrison. The records for 1826 show that a Master Patrick Cosgrove was the master, on a salary of between £15 and £26 annually. The school had twenty-two Protestants and ten Catholics at it. The Revd W. Vandeleur and the Revd J. M. Graydon were involved in management. There was some sort of disagreement and another school was opened. The ordnance survey of 1830 stated that there was a schoolhouse at the north extremity of the village at the expense of the incumbent, who gave four pounds annually towards the headmaster's salary.

In 1832 the Government established a system of National Schools in which all religions were educated together, being taught the same curriculum, except for Religious Education. In the spring of 1832, a National School was established in Newtownbutler. It was a single storey, thatched schoolroom, measuring 26½ feet x 14 feet, with a wooden floor. It was situated just behind where the Statue now stands at the entrance to St Mary's Roman Catholic Church. The Master was Mr Patrick Cosgrove.

The school established by Revd W. Vandeleur continued to operate under the control of the Church of Ireland until it was taken over by the National Board of Schools in 1877. It became Newtownbutler II National School from 1 August that year. The Principal was Mr Samuel Shields and Abegail Shields was assistant. Thomas Allen of Kilgarret was the first boy recorded on the Register of The National School and Margaret Allen was the first girl.

In 1919 the field at the rear of the school was purchased as a playing field from the estate of Lord Lanesborough. Some of the correspondence relating to this deal is preserved in the present primary school.

In 1941 the school was fully transferred to Fermanagh Regional Education Authority. Shortly afterwards, a large tree fell on the building and plans had to go ahead to build a new school. The new school was built by Short Brothers and Harland in Belfast and brought to Newtownbutler in sections. The local contractor was Mr George Carson. The new school was opened by the then Minister of Education, Mr Midgely in 1953.

The modern building, with so much glass, was quite a talking point in the area for a long time.

On the day of the opening only some of the pupils were allowed to attend, but the following day all the junior pupils were marched up to see the new school and were given the leftover sandwiches and cakes from the festivities of the day before. Master Harris was on duty with the cane to make sure that no one over indulged, was greedy or dropped crumbs.

One feature of the new school, which provided great interest, was the drinking fountain in each toilet area. There were continuous streams of pupils lining up to drink from them. This was at a time when very few houses even in the town had running water. The mains supply from Lough Narye was only being installed at that time.

The following is a list of teachers in Newtownbutler (II) Primary School since 1877.

Year	Principal	Assistants
1877	Samuel Shiels	Miss Abegail Shiels
1880	Mr Pillors	
1883	Mr Hugh Hobson	
1892	Mr Samuel Clugston	
1917	Miss Clara McDonald	
1920	Mr Richard H. Harris	Miss Janet E. Thompson
1935	Miss Florence M. Martin	
1936	Miss Vera McCarrisons	
1936	Miss Lena Ingram (Mrs Mount)	
1953	Miss Marjorie Hall (now Mrs Burke)	
1955	Miss G. Little (now Mrs Siberry)	
1957	Mr Joe Montgomer	Miss Ada Bussel (Later The Revd) 3rd teacher (now Mrs Kerr)
1961	Miss Edith Dixon (Mrs Douglas)	
1973	Mrs Louie Rutledge	
1976	Miss Trudy Morgan (now Mrs Taylor)	
1976	Mrs Ada Kerr	
1985	Miss Ruth Wilson (4th Staff)	
1988	Mr William Little	
1998	Mrs Jennifer Dunne	

Newtownbutler National School situated at the entrance to the present Roman Catholic Church continued in operation until 1934 when a new school was built on the site of the present St Mary's Primary School. The 1934 school was renovated and enlarged in 1974.

The most recent headmasters were Mr G. McCormack, Mr T. Doherty, Mr G. Brooke, Mr D. O'Hare, Mr P. McGilly, Mr Thomas Gunn and Mr Frank Maguire (2003).

Of the many small schools in the countryside round Newtownbutler, only one is still in operation — namely St Joseph's, Donagh, which was built to replace a school at Ballagh.

The rest of the small country schools have closed and most of the pupils now transported to Newtownbutler by bus.

Schools, which have closed include; Feaugh, Drummully, Wattlebridge, Clonmaulin, Derryginnedy, Tiraffy, Gubb, Crom and Magheraveely.

The present Orange Hall at Feaugh, which has recently been renovated, was the former Feaugh Primary School. It closed about 1924. The last teachers were a Mr J. W. Thompson and his daughter. Some of their relatives still live in the area.

Drummully School closed in 1957 and the pupils transferred to Newtownbutler.

The list of teachers in Drummully from 1860 is as follows; Mr Glendinning, Mr Coulter, Mr Lyons, Miss Fanning, Miss Patter, Mrs Talbot, Miss Mackey (Mrs Thompson), Miss E. Curry (Married Revd G. Perdue, later Bishop of Cork), Miss Kennedy, Miss Wilson, Miss Rolston.

Midhill, as it was known locally, or Magheraveely Primary School to give its proper name closed in 1977 and its pupils went to Aghadrumsee. The teachers in service when it closed were Miss Fleck and Mrs Hicks.

Tiaraffy School near Sallaghy, where Mrs Kennedy and Mrs Hall taught, closed in 1978 and some of the pupils came to Newtownbutler.

There was a school at Crom, which closed in the 1950s. The pupils had to be taken by 'cot' to and fro across the Lough to school. Rowing the cots across was a difficult and tiring job in winter weather. In the 1930s someone was drowned on the journey and only after that incident was a lifebelt carried on the boat. When the school closed, the pupils cycled to Newtownbutler or Teemore. Later a bus was provided.

Revd J.C. Taylor

The Revd J.C. Taylor, Rector of Galloon from 1916 to 1940, contributed much to the education of many people in the Newtownbutler area. He provided a selection of books in the vestry of the church. Parishioners could borrow these and read them. This was of course in the days before mobile library vans. He is probably best remembered in the area for his school. He coached pupils for university and college entrance exams and for scholarship exams in a wide variety of subjects. He was by all accounts a great scholar himself and there are many people who can testify to his teaching ability by what they are today. There was no religious discrimination and his pupils came from all denominations.

On Saturday afternoons he ran a class for candidates for the Bishop's Medal Exam. This would have been for Church of Ireland teenagers. It wasn't 'all work and no play', because I have heard of one years study ending with a trip on a cruiser from Knockninny.

Revd J. C. Taylor, who died in July 1940, is buried in Galloon churchyard, Newtownbutler. His grave is marked by a celtic cross.

Music Teachers

Down through the years there have been several music teachers in the area. One of the first was Miss Moore, a sister of Mr Charlie Moore who established Wellworths in Enniskillen.

Miss Jean Moffatt has for many years taught piano at her home, Eden Cottage, Bridge Street. Children come from all over to benefit from her vast experience.

The late Mrs Margaret Boles taught piano at her home near Magheraveely. She moved to Lisnaskea around 1970.

Derryginnedy School in the early part of the twentieth century

Drummully Church of Ireland School, 1919-1920

Mrs Louie Rutledge, a former teacher at Midhill Primary School and Newtownbutler Primary School, takes some pupils from the Magheraveely area for piano lessons.

As the demand for piano lessons increased and the usual teachers were unable to cope, Mrs Eva Johnston began to take pupils. She has quickly established herself as a capable teacher and her pupils have achieved good results in various exams.

eighteen

The Art of Smuggling

Since today the Border Customs Stations are closed and the frontier between the Republic of Ireland and Northern Ireland is open to free trade as part of the European Single Market, it is perhaps appropriate to recall the practice of smuggling in the Newtownbutler District.

The roots of this practice go back to the 1930s when the British Government placed an embargo on the sale of cattle from the Irish Free State to the United Kingdom. Farmers south of the Border were being given little or nothing by the Free State Government in the way of subsidies for their cattle and so the option to sell to the smuggler was always a temptation. As there was also an Imperial preference for Northern Ireland cattle it meant that cattle bought cheaply in the Free State and smuggled over the Border would make a generous profit for the purchasers. Generally the Free State dealer would bring cattle to the Border where their Fermanagh buyer would take over. The Border town of Belturbet, County Cavan seems to have been one of the main centres for planning these clandestine operations. The cattle would often be bought cheaply at fairs throughout County Cavan and County Leitrim. The smuggling of cattle began as darkness fell and often the cattle were made to swim across Lough Erne on to one of the Islands in Northern Ireland. They were then driven across the island and then had to swim once again until they reached the northern mainland. It was said that the smugglers paid no heed to the weather conditions and that their only anxiety was the prospect of being caught by the police and excise men.

The smugglers were thought to have sent young boys ahead in the guise of fishermen and rabbit hunters to spy out the territory and to give the all clear.

The Royal Ulster Constabulary had a patrol boat moored at Bunn Bridge on the road from Newtownbutler to Crom Castle.

These 'young scouts' had various methods of 'tipping off' the smugglers. Red flags would be placed on hilltops or trees during the daytime and after dark flashlights and various sounds were used according to prearranged codes.

The Royal Ulster Constabulary often received advance information of cattle movements and would be lying in wait for the smugglers, some of whom were captured along with the livestock seized, while others made good their escape to smuggle another day. The RUC also visited the Border farms to take stock of the number, breed and colour of the livestock, as farmers, particularly on the Islands, acquired Free State livestock which were subsequently sold to the northern smuggler. If the farmer's alibi was not adequate upon being questioned by the Police or Excise men, the animal was usually disowned as a stray and subsequently impounded. The loss of a few cattle was preferable to the risk of prosecution.

In the war years, the *Impartial Reporter* carried a story of how Police from Newtownbutler surprised two men on the banks of the River Finn, on the Fermanagh/Monaghan Border, carrying loaves to a 'cot' used for transporting cattle across the River. One man ran away across the fields. The other took off all his clothes and with his pants around his neck, plunged into the River and swam the thirty yards to the Free State. Both men made good their escape. The Police seized all the loaves in the 'cot' and also found a jacket, boots and all the other clothing, except the swimmer's pants!

It was in the war years that smuggling increased for a number of reasons along the Fermanagh Border. The rationing of food, clothing and many other essential goods during the Second World War led to the increase of smuggling, particularly of sugar, butter, spirits and certain luxury goods still available in shops in the Irish Free State. For people living in Newtownbutler, Clones became a 'mecca' at this point in time. As the Free State was a neutral country, commodities such as flour and tea, which were scarce in southern Ireland, were smuggled by every conceivable means of transport.

Smuggling, therefore, was a two way process at this time. The smuggler, therefore, began what could be described as a two way 'shuttle service' as he frequently delivered flour and tea to the south and returned north with butter and sugar. The train journey to and from Clones seems to the present day traveller something of an adventure. The stories are numerous. Ladies would arrive in Clones with slim figures and leave some hours later looking as if they had put on quite a lot of weight and would walk past Customs Officers who first smiled knowingly and shook their heads as they let them go past unhindered. It was a continuous battle of wits between smugglers and Customs Officers as they tried to control the flow of contraband. The officers tended to turn a blind eye to small time or occasional operators but went all out to catch the larger parties.

After the war years, smuggling continued and at one stage, practically everything was being brought illegally over the Border from the Republic of Ireland, including lorries, cars, vans and goods of all kinds. One interesting story from the 1960s concerns a plan to bring a lorry load of alcohol, which was then much cheaper in the Republic, especially for the twelfth of July celebrations. The truck was spotted travelling along a Border road in the Newtownbutler locality and the customs gave chase. As they were catching up, the driver made a desperate effort to off load his cargo onto the road in front of the Customs' car. He failed and the chase continued until the lorry crashed over the hedge into a field. However, as was the habit and good fortune of smugglers, the driver made his escape. The load of drink was estimated to have been worth around £12,000, a large sum at that period of time.

The Border is now open but the mystic and romanticism of smuggling still lives on in the hearts and minds of many in the Newtownbutler area.

nineteen

The War Years
(1939-1945)

Memories

Some who remember the war years, recount travelling to school on trains which ran to Enniskillen and on to Londonderry. The windows of the trains were netted with sticky tape to prevent the glass shattering in the event of an air raid. The light bulbs were blue in colour so that trains would not be so obvious to flying enemy aircraft. Town lights were not allowed and at night, house lights were not to be visible from the outside. Even torch lights had to be minimised. This whole process was known as the 'blackout'.

Gas masks were provided for everyone and had to be carried at all times. These were fitted for the public in the Courthouse by trained helpers.

Various battalions of soldiers were housed at Crom. These included; The Seaforth Highlanders, The Berkshires and American Infantry. Mr Frank Marshall, the late husband of Mrs Sarah Marshall of High Street, served with The Seaforth Highlanders. The whole estate was scattered with Nissan huts for the soldiers and the Officers lived in the Castle. Many in Newtownbutler gave hospitality to these men; some remember making steak-and-kidney pies and chips to feed them. Tennis was played on Chapman's lawn at Lurganboy.

On a hill, along a little road from Mullanahorn Bridge, in the townland of Killyroo, the R.A.F. ground staff had a radio station. Radio location was in its infancy. It is said that this station was involved in the land and air communications with the Catalina Flying Boat, which flew from Castle Archdale, which first located the German battleship 'Bismarck'. This sighting resulted in her being sunk. The anchor belonging to this flying boat is on permanent display in Fivemiletown High School.

E.N.S.A. (Entertainment's National Service Association) Shows used to come and perform for the R.A.F. and Army stationed in the area. There were dances in the Courthouse for the Army and Air Force personnel. Some of the American Forces lodged in Reilly's Hotel (Lanesborough Arms). Local people were encouraged to attend the entertainment functions.

At this time, petrol was severely rationed and only a few people had cars. Doctors and Clergymen had priority. Many other things were rationed. There were coupons for butter, margarine, sweets and clothes, to name but a few. Rationing continued until the fifties.

Modern Main Street, Newtownbutler

The Old Parochial Hall (Church Hall)

There was a canteen in the Old Parochial Hall (Church Hall) for the forces. Mrs Hamilton Johnston and the late Miss Molly Johnston helped to organise it.

The former Bishop of Clogher, the Rt. Revd Robert W. Heavener, then Rector of Irvinestown, was Chaplain to the forces stationed in County Fermanagh and was also the Army Welfare officer.

There was no television in those days, wireless kept us up-to-date with the news. It is widely believed that the first wireless receiver in the village of Newtownbutler was assembled by Mr Cormac Reilly (later Doctor) and Mr Jack Allen. Wireless, in those days, was normally powered by the use of dry and wet batteries, the latter requiring frequent recharge. It was a common sight to see people carrying the batteries to the local garage for re-charging. During this time, unless one had the luxury of having two wet batteries, reception of wireless transmission was not possible.

The Home Guard was a local group of men from each area, who wore a uniform when on duty, to defend the area from potential enemy action and kept a general lookout. Mr Jack Alien and Mr F. J. G. Chapman were Home Guard Officers.

Mr Packie McNamee was the local barber of the day who acted as hairdresser for the Army and R.A.F. He was also active in a little barber shop opposite the Orange Hall in Main Street.

After the War, many surplus military aircraft were stripped of aluminium. This salvaged material was subsequently reprocessed and used in the construction of emergency housing schemes. Examples may still be seen in various parts of the county and currently at the Newtownbutler Controlled Number II Primary School.

twenty

Recreational Pursuits

It seems that there were few youth organisations in Newtownbutler before the beginning of the twentieth century, except for the G.A.A., which was already in existence at this time. The G.A.A. is discussed in more detail in the following chapter. One of the first youth organisations may well have been the Church Lads' Brigade. Ernest Johnston was one of the members who was given a Certificate on 30 October 1926. The Revd J. C. Taylor was the Chaplain. Mr Harry Sewell was the Drill Instructor.

Mrs Stothers organised the Girls' Friendly Society about 1940.

In 1953, the year of the Coronation of Queen Elizabeth II, Mrs Louie Rutledge formed a company of Guides. During the following years various people served as Guiders. Although the names are not in chronological order, these Guiders includes; Mrs Sally Johnston, Mrs Lena Shiels, Miss Ruby Kettyle (now Mrs Rountree), Miss Violet McCartney (now Mrs Duncan), Miss Lorna McCoy (now Mrs Benson), Miss Joyce Marshall (now Mrs Armstrong), Miss Laura Bell (now Mrs Irvine), Mrs Joan Johnston (née West), Miss Lorna Hutchinson (now Mrs Elliott), Miss Jennifer McAllister and Mrs Yvonne Bowles (née Johnston).

The Brownies were started by Miss Primrose Morgan (now Mrs Robinson) and Miss Georgina Kettyle (now Mrs Johnston). Later Mrs Louie Rutledge took over the leadership. She was followed by Mrs Bonnie Latimer, Mrs Gladys Bell, Miss Heather McCartney (now Mrs Nixon), Mrs Freda Alien, Miss Margery Armstrong and Miss Minnie Godfrey.

Sea Scouts were started by Commander Crichton of Crom and the Revd Nevil O'Neill.

The Scouts were started by Mr Ronnie Kemp and the late Robin Bell and the Cubs were started by Mr Derek Woods and Mr Billy Talbot. Other leaders were Miss Lorraine West, Mr John Allen, Miss Margaret Johnston (now Mrs Jordan) and in 1988, Mr William Little became the Cub Leader and was later assisted by Mrs Hazel McVitty.

The Rainbow Guides were founded by Mrs Janet Baylor in the autumn of 1990. The assistant leaders were; Mrs Linda Phair and Miss Paula Shiels, who were later joined by Mrs Betty Darling.

The Roman Catholic Guides were started in 1983 by Dympna McAvinney, Caroline McDermott, Patricia Beattie and Rosaline Maguire.

The Roman Catholic Scouts were started in 1982 by Mr Jimmy McPhillips (now the Revd) and Mr Martin Taggart.

The Cubs - started by Mr Derek Woods and Mr Billy Talbot

Badminton was played in the Courthouse, now The Community Centre, before the war and also in the Old Church Hall before its renovation. Now Badminton is played in both the New Church Hall and in the Roman Catholic Parochial Hall.

There used to be several tennis courts in the town, one was at the Rectory, another at Dr Dolan's house, along the Church Lane and one at Chapman's. Dr Fitzgerald had both a hard court and a grass court. There were also courts at the larger houses in the vicinity, including Crom Castle. Long ago the streets were lined with carriages (horse drawn) to bring the players to play at each other's houses.

Bowls are played in the Church Hall and bingo is played in the Roman Catholic Hall.

The Women's Institute was started in 1966.

The Mother's Union was started in the late 1950s by Mrs Maud O'Neill and was revived by Mrs Hay about 1982.

A popular outdoor pastime in the area is hunting. A group of men gather with their hounds to chase a fox or hare over the fields. The men follow on foot. Occasionally a dead fox is dragged round a course and the hounds released to follow the scent. This is called a drag hunt.

Often after a hunt, the huntsmen adjourn to a public house to discuss the events of the day or sing about it, led by John Maguire.

twenty-one

The Gaelic Athletic Association in Newtownbutler

The Early Years

It is thought possible that gaelic football of some sort was played in the Newtownbutler area prior to the formation of the Gaelic Athletic Association in 1884. Official records do, however, confirm that, in 1887, over one hundred years ago, the first Gaelic Football Club in County Fermanagh was founded in Newtownbutler by three gentlemen — Master Maguire, the principal of the Roman Catholic Primary School of the day, Barney McManus and Philip Brady.

The local Club was aptly named the 'Newtownbutler First Fermanaghs' and the playing panel consisted of about twenty-one players.

The earliest recorded writings of this team is of them taking part in a tournament in Belturbet in 1888. The First Fermanaghs won on that day defeating the local Rory O'Mores, Armagh Sons of Uisneagh and Bawnboy Gallowglasses in the process.

The team on duty that day over one hundred years ago was as follows; Charlie McDermott, James Seattle, John Tummons, John McAdam and Thomas Conlon (Landbrock), James McManus, James McAviney and Pat McManus (Derrykerrib), John McMahon (Derryginniddy), Paddy Duffy (Gubb), Patrick McCabe and Phil Caughey (Feaugh), Paul Wilson, William Wilson, Alex Gribben, Michael McCaffrey, Phil Reilly, Patrick and Arthur Maguire (Derrygolan), Hugh Fitzpatrick and James McDonagh (Galloon), James Murray (Derrykenny), Patrick McDonnell (Gortbrannon), James McDonald (Drumhilla).

The team was a twenty-one-a-side and was captained by Phil Reilly, the son of a Ballyconnell stonemason, who was a grand uncle of two well-known Newtown and Fermanagh stars of the 1950s, Joe and Dermot McCormack.

Transport at the time took the form of two or four old flat wooded boats, which were used at that period for transporting cattle to and from the islands.

An Irish Folklore Collection of 1887 gives an account of the formation of the First Fermanaghs by a Club member, Frank Conlon of Landbrock.

The jerseys were green and white stripes tasseled caps of the same colours and white moleskin breeches. They played with the new 'big' football, which came from Dublin. Big strong men were the order of the day. Point posts were placed on either side of the goal posts and the cross bar was a simple 'hairy-ned' rope.

The man known as 'The Charger' was placed near the opponent's goals and when he caught the ball the players shouted 'rush' and every effort was made to bundle man and ball past the goalkeeper.

Around this time the G.A.A. came into opposition with the church authorities and this, no doubt, led to a decrease in the number of clubs and until about 1904, there appears to have been very little football activity. During this time, we find the 'Donagh Sons of Erin' to the fore around 1909 and some of their players later played with the 'Newtownbutler Brehons' in and around 1915, 1916 and 1917.

When County Fermanagh played County Cavan in 1910, the McGarvey brothers, Mick and Tommy, along with Dan McQuillan played for County Fermanagh. A team called the 'Wattlebridge Eire Og's' came into prominence after this period and we find them contesting the 1912 Fermanagh Championship Final against the 'Teemore Shamrocks'. Wattlebridge lost this game, which wasn't surprising, as Teemore were well known as the leading team in the County at this time, inspired by the Clarke brothers.

Teemore also defeated the 'Newtownbutler Brehons' in the 1915 and 1916 County Championship Finals but had fallen to the Brehons in the 1914 League Final.

The 'Newtownbutler Brehons' of that period included such great stalwarts as Dan McQuillan (Capt.), Mick McGarvey, F. Meehan, C. Colgan, Comdt. Matt. Fitzpatrick, F. Murray, S. Egar, J. McNamee, W. McGarvey, Tommy Murray, J. Fitzpatrick, E. McAdam and Capt. J. McKenna.

Wattlebridge contested all four County Finals from 1917 until 1920, losing the first two to Teemore and Irvinestown respectively and defeating Irvinestown and Derrylin respectively in the last two years. The backbone of this Wattlebridge side comprised of Matt. Fitzpatrick, Mick McGarveny, F. Tinnenny, Frank Meehan, T. Wilson and T. McGarvey.

Wattlebridge also beat Teemore in the 1926 League Final.

The next success came in 1924 in the Junior Football League when Newtownbutler, playing under the name of 'St Aidan's' defeated Kinawley. They lost the following year in the Final to a Derrylester team.

St Aidan's won the 1934 Senior County Championship, defeating Irvinestown in a thrilling Final in Enniskillen. Some of the St Aidan's panel of that Final were as follows; James Eddie Naan, Frank McGahern, Phil Swift, 'Red' Tom Wilson, Jack Connolly, Patsy McPhilips, W. McGarvey, Bennie Reilly, Willie Buchanan, Hughie Fitzpatrick and the only surviving member is Hughie Reilly of Kilnacran, Newtownbutler.

Hughie Fitzpatrick was the father of 'Red' Hugh Fitzpatrick of Newtown and Beragh fame and grandfather of Mark, Paul and Hugo Fitzpatrick, present day stars with Newtown Youth and Senior Teams.

Hughie Reilly, affectionately known as 'Black Hughie', is a nephew of Tommy Murray of Starachan who starred with the Brehons in the 1914-1916 period. A grandson of Hughie is the up and coming Kinawley star, Martin McBrien.

In 1936, Wattlebridge again secured players from Newtownbutler and in 1937, won the Senior League, beating Enniskillen and finished runners-up in the 1938 Senior County Championship Final to the 'Lisnaskea Emmets', whose players included the great Frank Johnston.

The Golden Forties

Following representations made by the Parish Priest of Newtownbutler, Father Maguire, to Fermanagh County Board, most of Wattlebridge's players transferred back to Newtownbutler.

Newtownbutler now played under the name of St Comgall's and the transfer of players from Wattlebridge seemed to pay dividends because they reached the 1939 Senior Football Cup final, won the League and Championship Final in 1940, reached the Championship and League Final in 1942 and in 1944, won the Championship and reached the League Final.

This period in the 1940s was known as the 'Golden Forties' and Newtownbutler St Comgall's were served by players of the calibre of Eric McQuillan, Terry Donegan, Mickey O'Harte, Mark McDermott, Charlie McNamee, John Thomas Lynch, Benny Alien, Frank Murray, Eamonn Carey, Hughie Reilly, Tommy Martin, Dessie Leonard, Michael (Bert) Murray, Attie Maguire, Jimmy Mohan, Johnny Courtney, Benny McDermott, Peter Murray, Mickey McNamee, Francy Donegan and McCartan McAviney.

During this bright period in the Club's history, men like Eric McQuillan, Benny Alien, Terry Donegan, Mark McDermott and Peter Murray, amongst others, served their County as well as their Club.

The only remaining achievement of the forties was the winning of the 1949 Minor County Championship and several of those young boys went on to become Club and County Seniors in the 1950s.

The 1949 Minor Panel makes very interesting reading; Joe McDermott, Fergus McQuillan, Tosh Donaghue, Joe McCormack, Paddy Foster, Jim Dolan, J. Tummons, C. Fitzpatrick, Eddie McDermott, Ignatius McQuillan (later to be ordained to the Priesthood), F. Tummons, T. Teague, Dermot McCormack, J. Mullally, Brendan Shannon (later Father Brendan) and Charlie McLoughlin.

Trophies in the next couple of years were scarce but, in 1953, St Comgall's became County Senior Champions by defeating a gallant Irvinestown squad at rain soaked Enniskillen. This team included several of the 1949 Minors, including Ignatius McQuillan and Dermot McCormack. The 1953 success was to be the last until Newtownbutler ended the Roslea Shamrock's sequence of wins in 1959 by winning the Championship with a three point winning margin. Newtownbutler won the 1960 League Trophy by virtue of a good win over Derrygonnelly.

Players on this great Newtown team included; Fr Ignatius McQuillan, the O'Keefe's, the Caughey's, Patsy McKenna, the Connolly brothers, Eugene Donegan, Aidan McCarron, Fr Shannon, the Hueston brothers, Maurice McNamee, Vincent Sweeney, Johnny McCaffrey, Terry M. Gorman, the Murphy brothers, Eddie Crudden, John Wilson, Brian Wilson, Pat McKiernan and Philip Wilson.

The 1964 County Championship Final saw Newtown again contest the game with old foes, Devenish and it was Newtown's turn to bring home the New York Gold Cup. The players mentioned above had all played their part in securing the 1964 Championship and unfortunately, this was to be the last Senior Championship victory within the Club until the present time.

Official opening of St Comgall Park and club rooms

On Sunday 1 June 1986, the Most Revd Dr Joseph Duffy, Bishop of Clogher opened St Comgall Park and Club Rooms. A special booklet was published by St Comgall's G.F.C. to commemorate the day with messages from Eamonn McCabe, the Club Chairman, Bishop Duffy, Fr Murphy and others. The booklet also included a wide range of photographs and details of the Club's history. There was also an under-16 football challenge, a Junior Camogie challenge and a Senior Football challenge, running from 3.00 p.m. through at intervals until after 7.00 p.m. that day as part of the ceremonies which began at 2.00 p.m.

GAA - 1964 Senior Champions

The last historic victory which we can record by Newtownbutler was the 1988 Senior Football Championship victory which was very appropriate as it was exactly one hundred years after the First Newtownbutler victory by the 'First Fermanaghs' at Belturbet in 1888.

twenty-two

Memories of the Huntsmen

For this section of the book, we are entirely dependent upon the men who hunted in the Newtownbutler area over the past fifty years. Arthur Maguire and his brother, John, supplied most of the memories, which follow. Arthur, known to many as 'Attie', lived for many years with his father, Patrick, also a huntsman and who lived to the great age of ninety-one years.

In the early years, it was the hare and not the fox, which was hunted. Arthur made it very clear that the intention of the huntsmen was to save, rather than to kill the hare during the hunt.

Arthur attended Derryginnedy School and often, at 2.00 p.m. on a Wednesday, Arthur had to ask permission from Master O'Hanlon, to be excused from classes. Master O'Hanlon always knew why Arthur 'wanted off school' even before he had the words on his lips. The hunt season was and is from 1 October until 2 March each year. Arthur recalled that Saturday was the usual day for the hunt. Arthur and Jimmy Morgan of High Street often set off at 9.00 a.m. on Saturday morning with nine or ten hounds and crossed the lake from Crom Estate to Derryvore Quay and met another pack of hounds from Teemore. It would have been about 11.00 a.m. before the hunt started. The hares would be raised by 'beating the fields' with sticks. As soon as the hare had been aroused, it would run for miles across many fields with the hounds in hot pursuit, followed by the huntsmen on foot. Arthur said that they never knew exactly where the hunt would end once it had begun. The hare would sometimes travel in a very wide circle and come back to the same spot from which it had been raised.

When the first hare had been hunted, the huntsmen would 'beat for another hare' and hunt until darkness fell. The huntsmen often had great trouble in gathering all the hounds after the hunt and sometimes, they had to return the next day to round them all up. The huntsmen travelled light and often they carried food with them to eat while they journeyed. There was always a party at the end of each hunt, which lasted into the early hours of the following morning. It was recalled that from three to four quarter barrels of porter were often enjoyed at such sprees. Arthur spoke of returning to Newtownbutler at around 8.00 a.m. that morning and of how Jimmy Morgan and he often hid behind a hedge as his father, Patrick set off for early Mass.

There were many stories about Arthur's father, Patrick, known locally as 'Wee Paddy'. Patrick once 'set a hunt' at Highgate, off the Magheraveely Road, with another group of huntsmen from Killyfole. Arthur was himself only 'a caddie' at the time but recalls that he thought it was a Jack Lynch from Lammy who wrote a song to commemorate the occasion. We are grateful to Arthur for supplying us with of the 'Killyfole' Hunting Song. Arthur has given us four verses of this well-known song. There are, obviously, many more verses which other old huntsmen will remember: —

This hare she raced right through Gortraw and left the pack behind
Then turning quickly to the right, she travelled with the wind
Then back across Gortbrannon and out by Highgate Lawn
The Newtown dogs were in the front, so we cheered them every one.

Well the fun was only starting in a place called Tantybulk
It was here Ned Crudden cheered, for old 'Gay Lad' done the work
Straight over Ringavilla and round by Kilroot Hall
Then back through Knockmakegan, they chased her one and all.

Coming back across the bottoms, Ned give another skirl
He fired his cap in to the air, saying come on wee 'Comely Girl'
But going through Drummusky scrub like a bolt from out the blue
'Old Freedom' landed in the front and started for to view.

There were huntsman gathered there that day from Kilridd to Carnmore
back through Magheraveely and from Lough Erne's shore
Here's a health to bold Ned Crudden, of sportsmen he's a star
For with 'Wee Comely' he did bring the cup to old Loughgare.

On another occasion, Patrick Maguire was coming home with a load of hay when he came upon a hunt, which was pursuing a deer. This deer had been raised at Ratoal and had reached a hill at Drumcru where the deer was cornered at a thorny hedge. Patrick left his hay cart and on reaching the hedge, caught the deer by the antlers and in the ensuing struggle, rolled from the top to the bottom of the hill with the deer still in his grip. The deer was soon tethered and Dr Fitzgerald bought the animal for £2 and kept it for some time, despite the fact that it was said to have had quite a temper when approached at close quarters.

This wasn't the only occasion on which Patrick chased a deer. Arthur recalled another hunt when Mickey McKenna and his father had raised a deer at Drumclay and the animal headed for Crom through Corlatt, at a time when the area was flooded. On entering Crom Estate, Patrick and Mickey met the former Lord Erne. Paddy expressed the hope to Lord Erne that he wouldn't shoot the hounds. Lord Erne replied that he couldn't shoot any dogs without holding them for three days and that, in any case, this particular deer had been damaging his crops and he wanted rid of it. The hunt continued until the deer crossed from Inisherk to Derryvore and was shot at Kinawley later that night.

Arthur also recalled the first fox, which was seen in the Newtownbutler area. It was some fifty years ago and was seen at Donegans of Kilnakirk on a Saturday. The fox was raised the next day at Mullnahorn and was hunted across to Drumquilla and was heading for Pipershill. William Moore of Pipershill had a whippet, which covered the fox's path and turned it back in the direction of the oncoming hounds. The fox was eventually cornered, but put up an enormous struggle with one of the hounds before being put down with a blow from a stick. The stick in question belonged to William Moore who was very reluctant to lend it for this task, as it had come all the way from America. Mrs McAvinney of Crom Road bought the fox and had it stuffed to preserve it. The fox's preservation, however, did not last too long. Billy Stein of Drumcru had a very large spaniel who, on spotting the fox in McAvinney's shop window, jumped through the window and made off with the poor fox. Needless to say, Mrs McAvinney was not too pleased with the episode.

Arthur Maguire, who lives in Camphill Park, still travels to the hunts on a bicycle but he lets 'the young fellows hit the fields'. He says it isn't the same nowadays with cars being used, unlike the early days when everything was done on foot.

There is still an active hunt in Newtownbutler and the Drag Hunt, which takes place from 2 March to 1 October, is often held on Galloon Island. In fact, the All-Ireland Drag Hunt took place in 1991 in the Newtownbutler District, with a dog from Cork the eventual winner. However, when one listens to the old huntsmen, one feels that things will never be the same as in those earlier days when people had less and had to make their own entertainment with what little they had.

twenty-three

Social changes in Newtownbutler during the twentieth century

At the latter end of the nineteenth century, Newtownbutler was a hive of industry. As the dole and old-age pensions had not come into existence there was a great deal of hardship and people were glad of work to eke out a living. The town was the property of the Earl of Lanesborough and in 1880 it had been recorded that he expended a large sum of money on the improvement of the town including drainage, pumps, side-paths and buildings, all of which gave employment to local families.

Water supply

Water is essential to any community. There never was a water shortage in Newtownbutler, but the purity left much to be desired and the fact that it had to be carried from the source to the houses made people economise on its use. The houses, in most cases, before the 1970s had no bathrooms. Some had a zinc bath, which was used once a week in front of the kitchen range. This had to be filled with a kettle or boiler at the side of the range and emptied afterwards with a jug and bucket. Then the water was poured down an outside drain. Toilets were usually in an out-house and a wooden seat was placed over a drain. The seat had to be scrubbed and the drain disinfected at frequent intervals with lime. There is still one of these outside toilets at Lurganboy House, but happy to say that it is now used as a tool shed. After 1970 (approx.) most houses had proper bathrooms and inside toilets connected to the sewage system. At Lurganboy House there was a pump at the back of the house, which was connected to a well at the front gate. The well is still in existence but it is covered for safety reasons.

Lord Lanesborough had pumps installed outside the old Barracks and in 1990 Swifts refurbished the pump for drinking water. A pump was also installed at the junction of the Clones Road and Bridge Street. This was taken away when the water supply was converted to the Mains early in the 1950s. The piped water now comes from the reservoir on the Lisnaskea Road, near Mullnahorn Bridge. This reservoir is supplied from Killyfole Lough. This water supply has made a great change in the standard of living.

Before the Mains water supply came to the town, the cattle were taken twice a day to drink at the river in Bridge Street, which they approached down the paved slip way beside the bridge.

Bridge Street, Newtownbutler 2005

There is a spa well marked on the Ordnance Survey Map on Cahey's land at Mullnagowan on the Magheraveely Road. The water was taken by local people for health reasons. Recently, Mr Brownlee started bottling natural spring water for sale. Some people have cures for warts, sprains and other ailments. There is a wart well in the townland of Clonkee. Beside the well is a mug and a framed prayer hangs nearby.

Electricity supply

Light and heat are important commodities for our well being. For hundreds of years people burnt turf and coal and had oil lamps. The coal was imported and the turf was cut in the bogs. Following the discovery of the generation of electrical power, Mr McGilly operated a power plant along the Crom Road and supplied some houses with this 'magical' power for heat and light. This is thought to have happened sometime in the 1920s and was later replaced by Mains electricity in the 1940s.

Transport

Before the use of tarmacadam, road mending was done by local people with stones brought from local quarries carried by horses and carts. Some of the roads were 'darned' with oblong patches of stones, which had been broken into small pieces by men with hammers. The old coach road from Enniskillen to Dublin went through Lisnaskea past Manor Waterhouse and Burke's of Wattlebridge. The horses were changed at both of these houses. At Drumcru Cross there is an old milestone. These stones were placed strategically along the route so distance could be measured. The Irish mile is longer than the English mile. In the late 1940s more people could afford private cars and various people ran taxi services. These included; Mr Charlie Harper, Mr Benny Allen and Mr Tommy Reilly. Mr Jim Gould and Mr Hubert Good of Magheraveely had car hire services.

The Great Northern Railway Company employed a large staff. Mr Moore was the last Station Master to live in the Station House and his daughter, Miss Doreen Moore still lives there. Mr Moore made a violin, which was played on by Mr Charles Haberrelter, the conductor of the Colwyn Bay Municipal Orchestra in North Wales. Mr Johnny McLaughlin, a Customs Clearance Agent, was the much loved porter who looked after everyone's needs. Mr Phil Houston and Mr Eddie McAdam were the signalmen who worked the point and signals from a special cabin. The level-crossings were manned by families who lived in the gate-houses, among whom were the McLaughlins, the Gribbons, the Johnstons, the Sherrys and the Elliotts to name but a few.

The advent of the Border brought a new group of people into the community in 1922 and 1923. These were the men who worked for H.M. Customs and Excise. Some of these men had been in the Royal Irish Constabulary, the names, which come to mind, are Mr Lannen and Mr Murphy. Mr Barnard had been in the Royal Navy, Mr Wilson was formerly a Captain in the British Army, while Mr Chapman, the Officer in charge, came from London.

The Main Customs Clearance Office for the area was located beside the railway platform.

The Mullallys had a fleet of private lorries, which carried goods from the railway to their ultimate destination and vice versa. When the Northern Ireland Road Transport was formed, the private companies were no longer allowed to undertake private hire, but some of the employees found jobs with the new official Transport Body.

Mr Cassidy, who lived in Enniskillen, ran a bus service at the same time as the railways were in existence in the area. Mr Fred Doherty was the popular conductor who helped passengers in and out of the buses with their parcels, bicycles, boxes of one-day-old chicks and any other equipment. The buses were absolutely crowded because they were the only means of transport for many in those days.

This was a great convenience to many people but to others who had an appointment it was frustrating. In those early days the bus would have stopped by request anywhere along the route. This custom ceased when the Ulster Transport Authority took over and then passengers were obliged to use official stops only. Now most people have telephones. The first telephone exchange was located on the lane between Main Street and Galloon Church of Ireland. A few years ago a bigger exchange was built along the Crom Lane.

The Shops

The shops have always given employment to many people. In the past, Mr J. W. H. Johnston had a very large business, which sold drapery, feeding-stuffs for animals, groceries, hardware and coal. He had vans on the road, which visited outlying farms and residences which were a great convenience at the beginning and middle of the century before many people had cars. The Johnstons owned many houses in the town, which were gradually sold to the resident tenants. In the 1920s and 1930s Kate McKeever had a really old-fashioned shop on the corner of Main Street and Church Lane which always smelt of onions and leeks. She sold the best value of sweets for a penny. These were sold in newspaper 'pokes' (like a cornet). She also sold 'gob-stoppers', these were very large round sweets and once you had one in your mouth you certainly could not

The Railway Level Crossing (now a residence)

speak for the next half-hour! These wonderful sweets changed colour while you sucked them, so while you enjoyed them you were tempted to look occasionally to see what colour they were!

Many shops have changed hands through the years. The following names have appeared on butchers' shops; Beatty, Teague, McPhillips, Burke, Connolly, McAvinney and after this, Lyndon Read. Mr McAvinney had a drapery shop and grocery as well as an Undertaking business on Crom Road. This undertaking service is still continued by Mr McAvinney's nephews in the Newtownbutler area.

There were two grocery shops in the High Street, one owned by Mrs Martin and the second passed through several hands. Originally it belonged to McCoy's who sold it to J. W. H. Johnston, then it belonged to Bowles, Kerr, Ebbitt and later came into the ownership of Mrs Florence Creighton who had part of it converted into an Eating House with a cosy turf fire and Irish traditional memorabilia. Mrs Bussell and Miss Clerkin had drapery shops and Mr and Mrs Emerson had a general shop. Mrs Byron also had a shop and cooked dinners for passing travellers. Now, in Bridge Street, Eamon McPhillips has a thriving grocery business while Philip Swift and Dessie Courtney have filling stations with grocery shops attached. Mr Billy Coulter now owns the shop, which belonged to J. W. H. Johnston and Mr Jim Coulter has a well-stocked furniture shop in High Street. Mr Gabriel O'Keefe has a grocery shop also on Main Street. The Main Newsagent was John Nicholl whose daughter later succeeded him. The shop reminded me of illustrations from a fairy story. There were boots and clogs hanging over the counter which was so high a child could not see over it and like Mr Brady's, the shop had that wonderful aroma of leather. The shop was later sold to Gould's, then to Burke's, but managed by Jordan's and then owned by Mr and Mrs Ivan Wiggins.

'Lucky House' Chinese Takeaway - Main Street today

Along the Main Street, wear where Mr and Mrs Donaghy live, there was an old egg store, which was taken over by Bobby Crilly and Freddie Gardiner for a garage. Later they moved to the School Lane and eventually to the Crom Road, where the Creamery used to be. Some years ago this and Clarke's House were demolished. There is a garage at the back of Gray's shop on Main Street. Gray's shop was known for having well-dressed windows to attract the customers who like to invest in the latest fashions.

In her lifetime Mrs Gray organised several Fashion Shows for charity. Gray's shop was formerly Johnston's Cloth Shop. Johnston's Cloth Shop received a box of books once a month from the Library in Enniskillen. Now a Library van calls once a week. Cadden's and O'Donnell's had grocery shops along the Main Street, which are no longer in existence.

Hotels and public houses

There were two hotels in the town, one of which was The Lanesborough Arms, called after the famous Lord Lanesborough and attached to the hotel, was a public house and grocery shop. This group of buildings was built in 1820 by John Reilly, a stonemason from near Ballyconnell in County Cavan. John Reilly also built the Court House and the Market House (now the Church Hall) about the same time. 'The Tavern', as the pub was called, was subsequently owned by John Reilly's two sons, John and Philip.

In 1856 Philip Reilly was listed as a grocer, wine and spirit dealer and hotel proprietor in trades directories, but he died at an early age and the property eventually passed to Miss Rose Reilly who managed all three businesses until about 1956 when the hotel became a private dwelling. The present owner, Mr Dermot McCormack is a great-great grandson of the builder. He has the original account books dating from 1850 to the early 1990s. These ledgers offer an insight into the daily routine of business from the post-famine period to the advent of the motor car.

The frontage of the pub was taken to the Ulster American Folk Park, near Omagh, in 1987 and replaced by a replica made by the carpenter Albert Johnston. McQuillan's and Mulligan's, formerly the Railway Bar, are the two other public houses in Newtownbutler on Main Street. The second hotel in High Street belonged to Mrs Bussell and later to the Noble family and is the building where Mr Harry Sewell lives. It was called 'The Temperance Hotel' at one stage in its history. Mrs Ward had a guest house in Main Street in the building, which was the Doctor's Surgery until 1989.

Miss Mattie Lemon had a Lodging House and an Eating House on High Street from the 1940s onwards. There were a number of other eating houses in this period, which catered for farmers on Fair Days.

Post and banking

The Post Office used to be at the corner of Bridge Street and Main Street. Miss Forde was the Postmistress and later Mrs Sally Johnston succeeded her and moved the office to its present location. Mr and Mrs Mervyn Mills now own and run the Post Office on Main Street.

Newtownbutler 2005: The Lanesborough Arms Hotel

At one time the Northern Bank was only open two or three days in the week, the office at that time was in Farrell's front room where the old Post Office sorting used to take place. Afterwards the bank took over the house which had once been the Rectory on High Street.

The Ulster Bank opened a sub-office at the corner of High Street and Main Street opposite Reilly's Public House, but it later closed in the early 1980s. Mrs Hamilton Johnston and Mrs Cecil Burke told me about a newspaper called 'The Newtownbutler Herald' which was printed at the corner of Crom Lane and High Street, but when it published too much scandal it had to close down.

Health care

About 1948 the Health service came into existence and medical attention became Government controlled. Children were immunised at school against various diseases such as diphtheria, scarlet fever and tuberculosis, which curbed infant mortality. Vaccination against smallpox had been introduced sometime before this. The doctors in Newtownbutler included; Dr Duffy, Dr Fitzgerald, who was the dispensary doctor and Dr Dolan. Dr Dolan in his later years engaged several other doctors to help him, including Dr Frizzell, who became his son-in-law, his own son Dr Jim Dolan, his daughter Isolda and Dr Nora Casey. Dr Dolan was followed by Dr Reen. After Dr Reen's untimely death Dr Devlin took over the practice. In 1990 a Medical Centre was built on the Clones Road. Nurse McAvinney was a midwife who brought many of the older inhabitants into this world. At that time it was the custom for babies to be born at home, not in the hospital. Nurse McAvinney was the mother of Dessie and McCartan McAvinney who owned businesses in the town for many years.

For about thirty years there has been a chemist shop in the town, the first was opened by Mr Ignatius O'Neill in High Street, then it moved to the premises now occupied by the hairdresser, Mrs Kay McBrien and finally to the middle of Main Street. Mr O'Neill retired in 1989 and was succeeded by Mr Paul Hughes. Mrs Eileen Callaghan (née Courtney) has an excellent hairdressing establishment in Bridge Street. Strangely enough, the Courtney family had a Public House in the same building many years ago.

A dentist, Mr McKinney, came from Lisnaskea two days each week and practised in the late Benny Alien's front parlour, situated on the upper corner of Crom Lane.

Tradesmen

Many years ago Mr J. W. Johnston had a cooper business (barrel maker) at the back of Eamon McPhillips' shop. At one time there were four blacksmiths in the town, one was near O'Keefe's shop, the second at the back of Mr Sam McCoy's house, the third was where Mrs Joan Alien and Miss Margery Armstrong now live and the fourth was opposite Elliott's in the Crom Lane. The blacksmiths were very important people in the community because horses provided the only power of locomotion in the nineteenth century. Mr Brady was the cobbler. He had only one leg, having lost the other during the First World War. He lived in a cottage opposite the Roman Catholic Parish Hall and worked in a little shed built onto the cottage. While he was at work he wore a leather apron and the smell of leather in the little shed was a real delight.

Mr Ralph Johnston of Kilroot, the father of Samuel Johnston of High Street and Mrs Margaret Wilson of Camphill, was well known for making creels and baskets out of willow rods. He was regularly seen collecting and transporting his raw materials and finished products with his pony and spring cart.

Main Street, Newtownbutler

We have already mentioned John Reilly as a stonemason, but there must have been many more in the vicinity because there are several well-made walls about the town. Even the sides of the river at the bridge are faced with stone. The bridge itself was built of cut stone and the cattle-walk to the river is beautifully paved with slabs of stone. The boundary wall of St Mary's Roman Catholic Church was re-built while Canon Maguire was Parish Priest Houses of the nineteenth century were partly built of cut stone and brick. There was a quarry in the Rock Meadow near the Rectory, which was later levelled about 1985.

Mr Reilly and his son were tailors who lived in a house on Main Street, which was approached by stone steps, which are still there today. When Sir Anthony Eden came to stay at Crom, Mr Reilly made him a pair of trousers for country wear. Mr Bob Johnston, the father of Mrs Sarah Marshall of High Street, was a carpenter and craftsman of high standards, in spite of the fact that he had only one eye. Later Mr Albert Johnston, a very talented craftsman, came to live in Newtownbutler and he actually made a window for Clogher Cathedral, as well as wooden windows for Galloon Church of Ireland after the church was damaged in one of the bomb blasts. For many years Albert worked with the late Mr George Carson and later with Mr R. Robinson.

During the early 1950s a fire gutted some thatched dwellings located along Main Street (fortunately no lives were lost). Mrs Vincent Murray (née Wilson) was born in one of these houses, Mrs Jim Elliott (née Lang) lived there and a clog maker called Mr Henderson worked in one of the other cottages. The site was subsequently cleared of rubble and the Dixon family from Clones erected a garage thereon. An extensive business was conducted for a number of years. Later an extension was built on the same site to facilitate the manufacture of pre-fabricated type milking parlours known as the Somerset Milking Parlour. Many examples may still be found giving satisfactory service. These business activities were discontinued and the premises were converted into a lorry depot known as; Arrow Fast, Erne Freight and currently Target.

Mr Baker makes camogie sticks for many clubs in Ireland. His yard is beside the Paint Shop in the Main Street.

Fairs

The Annual Hiring Fair in Newtownbutler took place on 12 May. Men and women as young as fourteen years were hired as labourers or domestic staff for a period of six months. They were paid an agreed sum and received accommodation. The living conditions for these people were often harsh and the labour demanded of them severe. These men and women hired themselves out over a number of years as their source of income and livelihood. This often relieved larger families of the financial burden of feeding and looking after the older members of the family and proved to be the early training ground in work experience for many a young man or woman.

Smaller fairs were held once a month and Market Day was every Tuesday. These activities were organised by the Fairs and Markets' Committee. About the middle of the century, cattle grading was done in pens built at the junction of the Milltown and Clones roads. The Milltown road got its name from a flour mill, which was situated near where Alfie Hall lives.

Farming

Families, who lived in the town, bought milk for the local merchant and farmer, Mr J. W. H. Johnston. Tommy McManus was the Johnston's cattle drover who took cattle from the Lurganboy fields to be milked by hand in the farm yard. On the return journey, he supplied milk to some families. When the Johnston's retired from farming and let the land, people opted to fetch milk from Reilly's (of the Hotel).

Creamery carts, drawn by horses, collected milk from local farmers and took it to the creamery along the Crom Road, known as the Willow Park Creamery. Some farmers took their own milk to the creamery by farm cart. Horses and carts were later replaced by milk lorries. Mr George Nixon was the last Creamery Manager. Eventually the creamery closed and the Fivemiletown Creamery delivered bottled milk to the doorstep.

An example of some horse-drawn farm implements are on display in Mr Francis McNamee's garden on the Wattlebridge Road.

Haymaking methods have changed considerably too and seldom do we see the laps and rucks of hay in the fields or stacks in the haggard. During the war years the army helped the local farmers at harvesting season. Today, we see neatly bound bales, which are taken to the barns for storage. Silage has largely replaced hay for the winter fodder.

Flax was grown locally before 1950 and during the summer vacation students went to farms to help to pull the flax by hand. During the Second World War, flax was needed for the production of linen covering for aircraft.

Long ago farms were divided between the sons of the family and so holdings became smaller and smaller, but within the last fifty years farming methods have changed considerably. No longer are so many people employed on farms since the invention of tractors and milking machines, amongst others. Mrs Marjorie Burke of Wattlebridge has a medal, which was awarded to William Goggins by the Newtownbutler Farming Society for the best sow and litter in 1855. On one side of the medal it states 'Royal Agricultural Improvement Society of Ireland Instituted; AD 1841'.

Medal awarded to William Goggins in 1855

The Play Group, Newtownbutler 2005

The Poultry Club

The Poultry Club was started on 17 February 1959. There were twenty-six members, which increased to thirty in 1961. The aim of the Club was to improve the standard of poultry rearing and egg production. It met, in the now demolished Clarke's house, which stood at the cross roads beside the Community Centre.

There was a varied programme, talks were given on the new system of grading eggs in 1961 and the management of hybrid fowl production, another talk was on fowl pest control and the contemporary scheme for marketing eggs. In 1968 the minutes state that they had their first meeting after the restrictions of foot and mouth disease were lifted, so meetings were probably discontinued during this period.

In 1962 Mr Langham, who resided at Crom, gave a talk on his recent visit to East Africa. The Lisnaskea Club were guests.

At one time eggs were graded by Thompson's in what is now the Church Hall (see notes on the Church Hall) on High Street.

The Club also had its social activities. Outings were organised to the Balmoral Show, the R.D.S., Dungannon, Bangor, Crossfield Mills, Donegal, Butlin's, County Meath, Limerick and other places. In 1969 the Tenth Anniversary Dinner was held in Bothwell's Hotel in Lisnaskea. The cake was made by Mrs Maud North of Farm and decorated by Mrs Lena Shiels of High Street. Mrs Florence Hutchinson formerly of Mulladuff, made 'the hen and chicks', which were the symbols of the Club. The outing that year was to Mullingar, Longford and Bundoran.

In 1961 the subscription was 10 shillings and in 1972 it was 50 pence. In 1976 it was raised to £1.

The last entry in the minutes records an outing to Kesh in 1978.

Play Area Newtownbutler 2005

Newtownbutler today: 'New Faces' (Future Adult Child Education Scheme)

Initiatives

In 1968 there was a Newtownbutler Development Association; the annual subscription was 10 shillings (50p). Mr F. J. G. Chapman, Barbara Chapman's father, had his membership card signed by Mr Fergus McQuillan. In 1991, another Development Association representing all sections of the community was formed.

A survey was carried out in 1991 of the Newtownbutler area to assess the area for tourism, industrial development and general improvements. The idea of this was to present a viable proposition to various sponsorship bodies with a view to development in these areas for the benefit of the whole community. We look forward to seeing more changes for the better in the future in Newtownbutler district.

Conclusion

I hope that you have enjoyed reading this book and that you have found it informative and amusing in parts. When the book was started I wondered where I could ever find enough material to fill it, before it was finished it was almost a problem what to leave out. There is a wealth of local material to be had, if it could be coaxed out of people's heads and committed to paper. Perhaps this book will inspire some of you readers to share your memories with the present generation, to give them a flavour of the past. Too often we are accused of living in the past in this part of the world, but if we do not appreciate and understand our background, we cannot today respect the traditions of our fellow countrymen.

If this book, which is only the tip of the iceberg, as far as the history, culture and folklore of this area is concerned, goes only a little way to creating a better understanding of our heritage, then it has been worthwhile.

Much material of interest in the form of booklets, newspaper cuttings, postcards and photographs must lie hidden and undiscovered in boxes or cupboards or under the bed in many local houses. The value of such material is not in having it but having it displayed and shared with others. With modern reprographic techniques it is possible to have items copied and still retain the originals intact. I hope I have given you a taste of the interest and excitement that the use of such material can bring and might have encouraged you to share your knowledge of the area.

All over Ireland small groups of people have got together in historical societies, cultural groups, etc. to share a common interest in keeping alive the memories of an area. Is there the seed of such a group in this area? If this book is the starting point of such a group I will be delighted.

I have derived such pleasure from compiling this book. I have had the privilege and pleasure of talking to many interesting people. I have had an enormous amount of help and encouragement from a wide cross section of the community and I have learned much about Newtownbutler.

Thank you for reading the book and being interested in the story of a local community.

BARBARA CHAPMAN

Modern day Newtownbutler

Newtownbutler – an ever evolving Irish town!

Other titles published by Nonsuch

The History of Irish Cricket
GERARD SIGGINS

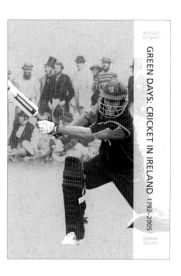

Irish cricket has a long, colourful history. The earliest photo of an Irish team is an 1858 team group of the Trinity 2nd XI. It was around this time that the game experienced a massive upsurge in interest – cricket was by far the most popular and widely played game in the country until the foundation of the GAA in 1884. By way of illustration, a recent history of cricket in Tipperary shows that at its height in the mid-1880s there were 98 clubs in that county alone. By the 1970s there were none. Designed to appeal to the casual and the hard core follower this book is a must for Irish Cricket fans. Gerard Siggins is the Assistant Editor at The Sunday Tribune and has been a writer and editor of several Cricket magazines over the years. Available October 2005.

1 84588 512 0

Voices of Trim
THOMAS MURRAY

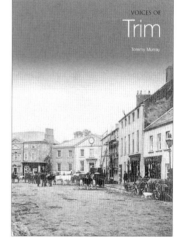

Compiled by locally renowned author and historical Thomas Murray this book focuses on the life and times of Trim in the past centuries. With interviews ad stories from and about the town and its hinterland's unforgettable characters and events it is a charm for any native and a beautiful introduction for the visitor or new arrival. Featuring snapshots of the changing lives and lifestyles of a provincial town and with an unrivalled collection of old photographs to accompany the text it is bound to have a wide appeal. Available October 2005.

1 84588 514 7

Tales from the banks of the Erne
JOHN CUNNINGHAM

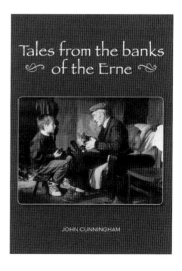

A place of great scenic beauty, Loch Erne has long been the inspiration for artists and draws tourists from far and wide. This is a unique collection of tales capturing the experiences and memories of people around the Loch Erne area through the last century, many of which have since passed away. These tales are charming in their humour and simplicity and touching in their honesty. John B. Cunningham is an Irish historian and writer born in County Donegal. He has been gathering and documenting the memories of the older people in the Erne area for some years now and this will form the basis of this enchanting book 'Tales from the Banks of the Erne'. The collection is illustrated with pictures of the tales many colourful characters. Available October 2005

1 84588 517 1

Dun Laoghaire Rathdown
PAT WALSH

Dun Laoghaire Rathdown sweeps from the Dublin Mountains down to the sea and this collection of over 200 archive images shows the area's heritage, history and people at their best. With pictures that recall the transport, leisure, and entertainment history of the county, alongside the everyday aspects of life this book will appeal to all Dun Laoghaire Rathdown's residents, young and old. Compiled by Dun Laoghaire Rathdown Librarian, Pat Walsh, these images provide a fascinating glimpse of life and the people of the area over the last century and more. Available June 2005.

1 84588 500 7

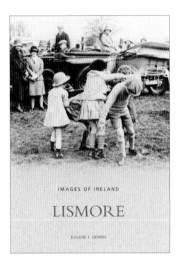

Lismore
EUGENE F. DENNIS

Lismore was founded in the seventh Century by St Carthage and takes pride in its history and traditions. This book captures the locals and the town at their charming best. It features a fascinating collection of some 200 archival photographs gathered as part of an impressive project by the author Eugene Dennis. Sure to appeal to locals and visitors alike. Available June 2005.

1 84588 501 5

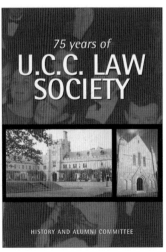

75 years of U.C.C Law Society
HISTORY AND ALUMNI COMMITTEE

Currently celebrating the 75 anniversary of its foundation, the Law Society has had a varied and interesting history. From its humble origins as a society created for the educated elite to its current manifestation as a college society active in organising charity, educational and departmental social events, not to mention its successful track record in debating and hosting many speakers of repute, the Law Society has changed as much as the society that surrounds it. Including many archive photographs and pieces by guest writers, this book outlines the changes, controversies and history of the Law Society since the 1920s. Informative and entertaining, this book will interest law students and alumni as well as those interested in Irish social history and the history of Cork. Available October 2005.

1 84588 513 9

We Are Rovers
EOGHAN RICE

Shamrock Rovers is Ireland's most successful football club and definitely the most recognisable of its soccer teams. It has an incredible record in terms of National League of Ireland titles and FAI cup victories. It has a considerable fan base regularly achieving attendance of 5-7,000 despite the fact that it has no fixed home-ground for the last few seasons while they await the completion of a new oft delayed stadium. Eoghan Rice is a successful journalist with the Sunday Tribune newspaper. He has been a fan of Shamrock rovers for many years and has rarely missed a game since he first attended a match at age nine in 1990. Available November 2005.

1 84588 510 4

A Class Apart The Gentry Families of County Kildare
CON COSTELLO

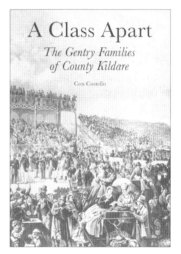

The landed gentry played a significant role in the history of Kildare. There has always been a deep fascination in 'The Big House' – the families living there, their treatment of the peasants, and their eventual fall. *The Gentry Families of County Kildare* is a fascinating exploration into the lives of a number of gentry families, their rise and their demise. Con Costello is well known in Kildare for his passion for history. He has been published on several occasions and edited the journal of the County Kildare Archaeological Society for some thirty years. *The Gentry Families of County Kildare* is a wonderful read from both an historical as well as a local point of view. Available November 2005.

1 84588 504 X

Athy Town
ROBERT REDMOND

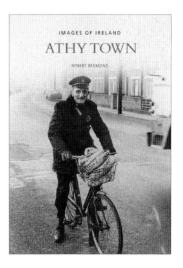

Athy is a sizeable and fast developing town in County Kildare. It is a designated heritage town and has a rich history dating back to the 12th century. Robert Redmond is well established as a photographer in his town and has taken photos all over County Kildare and Athy in particular. There are wonderful and varied pictures featured in this book. Social, religious and sporting events are illustrated, not to mention, the people and picturesque landscape of Robert's much loved town. Available October 2005.

1 84588 502 3

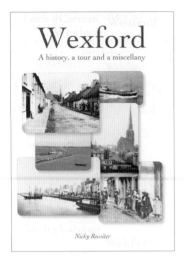

Wexford History Guide & Miscellany
NICKY ROSSITER

Nicholas Rossiter is a financial advisor working in Wexford. In his spare time he writes, produces and broadcasts a series of radio programs that combine Local History with Folk Music, a combination he find very effective and attracts contributions from across the world. He has been heavily involved in researching Wexford's History and has a considerable corpus of material at his disposal. Through this large body of material he takes the reader on a journey through Wexford's history and culture from early times to the present. Available November 2005.

1 84588 528 7

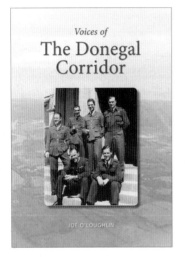

Voices of The Donegal Corridor
JOE O'LOUGHLIN

The Donegal Corridor, based along Lough Erne in County Fermanagh and up the Donegal coast, was a key contribution to the Allies in the Second World War. A place where ally soldiers trained for combat, where planes landed and refuelled and where many crashed and lost their lives. This intriguing book brings together a collection of memories, from home and abroad, of the Donegal Corridor. Joe interviews local people, family members and former comrades. The book is beautifully illustrated with pictures of many of these lost heroes, their aircrafts and the memorial sights of those who never made it home. This book will have a local as well as an international appeal. Available October 2005.

1 84588 526 0

If you are interested in purchasing other books published by Nonsuch, or in case you have difficulty finding any Nonsuch books in your local bookshop, you can also place orders directly through our website
www.nonsuch-publishing.com